HORSE
ANATOMY
for
Performance

Gillian Higgins
with Stephanie Martin

DAVID & CHARLES
www.davidandcharles.com

Contents

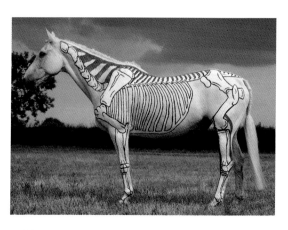

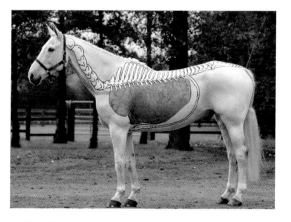

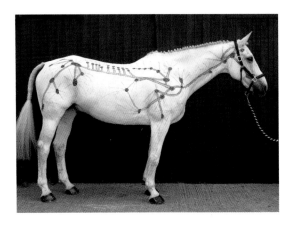

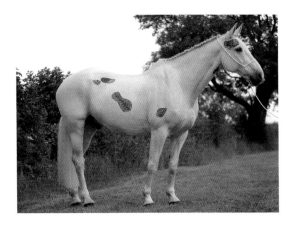

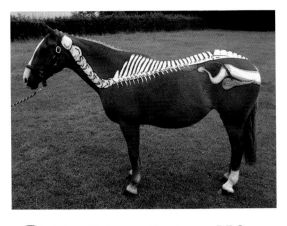

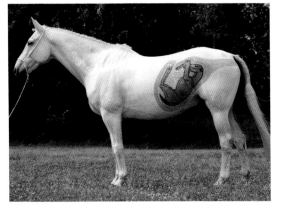

FOREWORD

by **Dr. Andrew Hemmings**
Neuroanatomist and principal lecturer in Animal Science and Production at the Royal Agricultural College

Fifty million years of evolution shaped the equine form to perfectly fulfil its biological function within a challenging ecological niche. On that basis the domestic horse is well equipped as a herd dwelling herbivore, able to survive on poor quality forage, with sufficient athleticism to outwit its prey. If we are to harness these attributes for leisure or competition purposes, horse keepers should gain a full appreciation of the various equine biological systems, and how they work in concert to maintain optimal health status. Previous books by Gillian have focussed primarily on anatomical characteristics of the musculoskeletal system. This most recent offering extends that information and also does considerably more. The 12 body systems of the horse and their interactions are presented in such a manner that always considers practical management and welfare applications. Furthermore, the beauty of the equine form, is once more illuminated and celebrated by Gillian's excellent painted horse illustrations. Indeed, it is a rare occurrence to find pleasing aesthetics and sound biological information in a single text. As such this most recent offering most certainly constitutes a logical progression for the *Horses Inside Out* concept.

Foreword by Dr. Andrew Hemmings

INTRODUCTION

The horse is a highly sophisticated living organism made up of atoms, molecules, cells, tissues, organs and systems. To enable him to reach his full athletic potential and give him a happy, healthy quality of life, it is up to us as carers, riders, trainers and therapists to ride him sensitively, manage him effectively, predict his emotions and behaviour, ensure that all his needs are met and give him the best possible chance to succeed.

To do this, it is important to understand both his capabilities and limitations within the context of his structure and function. The horse's body is a marvellous machine. Each anatomical system has individual tasks to perform but is also interdependent on each other. This book, a sequel to *How Your Horse Moves*, delves more deeply into how the horse functions and looks at some practicalities of anatomical training. Like *How Your Horse Moves*, it can be read as a whole or dipped into as required. Although there are suggestions for achieving desirable outcomes, it is not intended either as a training manual or a definitive anatomical text. It is designed to encourage the reader to study further, look at the horse in a new light, care for him with empathy and ride him with perception and consideration.

The skin, together with the hair,

hoof and various glands, make up

the integumentary system, which is

involved in protection and temperature

regulation, vital to health and survival.

The Integumentary System

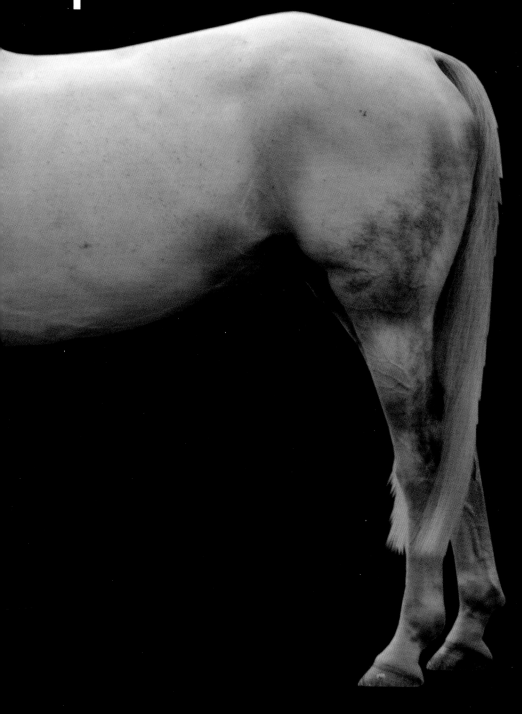

THE SKIN

The skin is a highly organised, complex system of nerves, tissue and cells designed to harmonise the horse's metabolism with his internal and external environment. Structurally, the skin consists of the epidermis and the dermis. It is the largest, heaviest organ in the horse's body. Its healthy condition is of **vital importance to health and survival**.

The epidermis is made up of several stratified layers of tough, non-vascular cells that vary in thickness. The layers can be likened to roof tiles overlapping. As the layers move up from the lower underlying living layer, they gradually die off and become toughened by a structural protein called keratin. The oil and sweat glands pass through the epidermis and reach the surface as pores. Vitamin D, synthesised in the epidermis following exposure to the ultra violet rays from the sun, is important for the absorption of calcium and for strong bones and teeth. Melanin, the pigment responsible for colour, also protects the skin from sunlight and is found deep within this layer.

The dermis is the deeper thick, live layer of the skin which is rich in blood vessels, nerve endings, lymphatic vessels, hair follicles and sweat glands. It is anchored to the hypodermis by an intricate network of collagen fibres, another structural protein, which give the skin its elasticity, suppleness and healthy appearance. Nerves in the dermis, together with hair follicles, act as receptors for touch, pressure, pain, vibration, tickling, warmth and coolness. Pain, when the skin is manipulated or exposed to temperature extremes can be an indication of impending or actual tissue damage.

Within the dermis there are two main types of gland:

- The **Sebaceous glands** which are located in the dermis and attach to each hair follicle. They produce sebum, a mixture of fats, cholesterol, proteins, salts and pheromones. Sebum coats the hairs to prevent them from becoming dry and brittle. It also prevents excessive evaporation of water from the skin keeping it soft and pliable and inhibiting the growth of certain bacteria.
- The **sweat glands** which release their secretions onto the surface of the skin through millions of pores.

The hypodermis is a layer of loose connective tissue which allows the skin to move freely. Subcutaneous fat is stored here. This provides insulation, is an energy store and acts as a cushion between the dermis and the muscle which, in turn, attaches to underlying tissues and organs. The hypodermis also contains large blood vessels that supply the skin. This region together with the dermis contains nerve endings that are sensitive to pressure.

SKIN MOVEMENT

The panniculus carnosus is a thin sheet of subcutaneous muscle that attaches to and interweaves with the skin around the trunk of the horse. It is responsible for moving, wrinkling and dimpling the skin. When the sensory nerves in the skin or hairs are stimulated by the tickle of a fly, for example, nervous messages pass directly to the panniculus carnosus causing it to contract and twitch the skin. This is well worth remembering when a horse does not respond to the leg!

This muscle only extends as far as the knee or hock and is not present in the neck. This means that when a fly irritates the skin on the lower legs, the horse will stamp his hoof or, if it lands on the neck, he will shake his head. This has been cited as a contributory factor in head shaking.

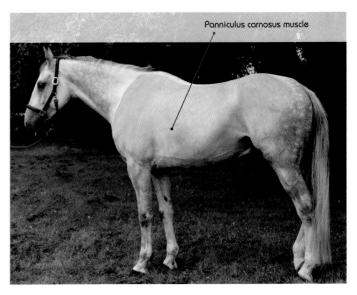

Panniculus carnosus muscle

Cross-Section of the skin

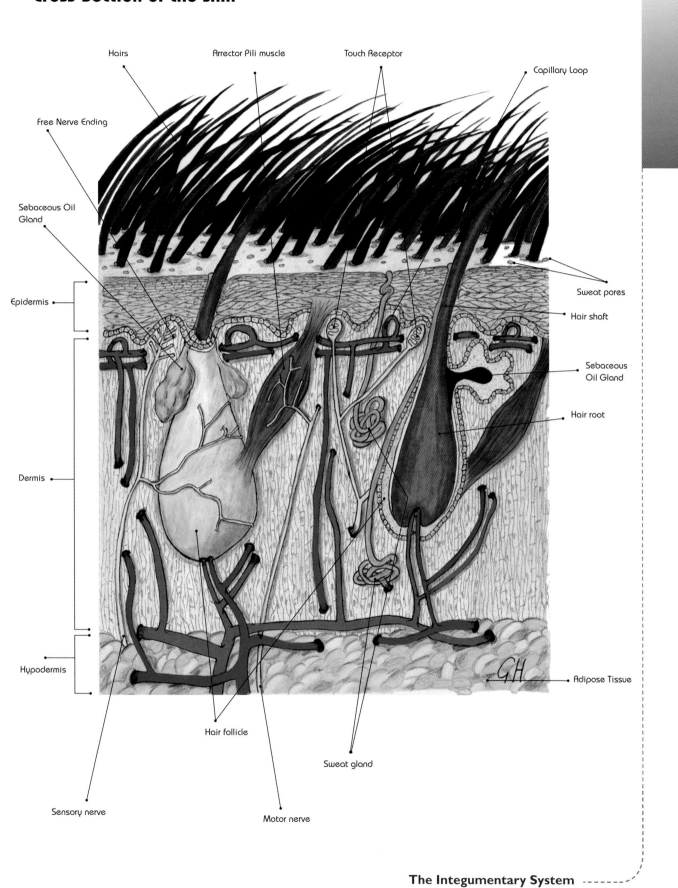

Hairs

Arrector Pili muscle

Touch Receptor

Capillary Loop

Free Nerve Ending

Sebaceous Oil Gland

Epidermis

Dermis

Hypodermis

Sweat pores

Hair shaft

Sebaceous Oil Gland

Hair root

Adipose Tissue

Sensory nerve

Hair follicle

Motor nerve

Sweat gland

THE HAIR

Hair originates in the dermis and is set at an angle. Each hair is a cuticle made of dead cells bonded together with protein. It has a **shaft** that grows from the **root**, which is surrounded by a hair **follicle.** Sebaceous glands secrete oils into the hair follicle, nourishing the hairs and creating a healthy shine to the coat. This is particularly evident in darker coloured horses. The oils also provide extra insulation and **grease** the coat to make it more waterproof.

There are three types of hair:

• **Permanent hair** – the mane, tail, eyelashes and feathers.

• **Tactile hair** – used to estimate the distance between the muzzle and an object. Especially relevant when the horse needs to locate an object.

• **Temporary hair** – consists of an undercoat of fine, densely packed hair, covered by a layer of longer, coarser hairs. This hair undergoes three phases in its life cycle, the growth phase, the transition phase and the quiescent or inactive phase, which ends with the twice-yearly moult triggered by hormonal changes, day length and temperature. During the growth stage, new cells are continuously being added to the hair follicle. When they die, they are pushed upwards, causing the hair to grow longer. In time growth stops and the resting stage begins. After inactivity, a new growth cycle begins to push the old hair root out of the hair follicle growing a new one in its place.

THE FUNCTION OF THE SKIN

Protection

The skin serves as the primary physical, chemical and biological barrier against weather, injury, dehydration and infection. It is also involved in controlling fluid balance, stabilising blood pressure and giving flexible support to the horse's body. The skin varies in thickness over the body depending on breed, age and sex. This makes some areas more sensitive than others. On the back, for example, it is denser and tougher than on the inner surfaces of the limbs where it is not as exposed. Around a joint, extra sebaceous glands make it more pliable. The skin is water resistant and cannot become waterlogged or completely dry out. The naturally acidic pH value of the skin inhibits the growth of micro-organisms and bacterial chemicals and can kill surface bacteria, fungi and viruses. It is also responsible for excreting some waste products.

The pigment melanin within the skin provides protection from the sun's rays. Horses with a white nose or snip are prone to sunburn.

Communication

The hair offers **protection** against grazes, bacteria, foreign bodies and the sun's rays. Touch receptors in the follicles are activated whenever a hair is moved even slightly. This means that horses are extremely sensitive to touch.

Sebaceous glands secrete oils into the hair follicle helping to nourish the hairs. These secretions develop grease within the coat adding extra insulation and shine and helping to make the coat more waterproof.

The skin is also responsible for producing chemicals that influence behaviour and attract the opposite sex.

Thermoregulation

Thermoregulation is the ability to keep body temperature within a certain range. The body temperature of the horse is 38°C. Sensitive nerves and receptors in the skin, skeletal muscle, abdomen and parts of the spinal cord send messages relating to body temperature to the hypothalamus – the thermoregulatory centre within the brain. (See page 112).

If the horse becomes too hot, through either high environmental temperatures or exercise, he deals with it in four ways:

1. **Evaporation.** This is the most effective way of losing heat. Sweat, secreted onto the skin, draws heat from the horse as it evaporates. As the core temperature rises through either external temperature or exercise, blood flow to the skin increases. About 60% of heat carried in the blood is transferred to sweat and is subsequently lost as the moisture evaporates from the skin surface thereby lowering body temperature. The cooling effect of sweating is significantly reduced in humid conditions where atmospheric moisture reduces the efficiency of evaporation. In these conditions the horse must be cooled quickly with copious amounts of iced water.

2. **Convection.** The air that passes over the horse's body is heated by the skin, rises and is replaced by cooler air, particularly if there is a breeze.

3. **Radiation.** The capillaries under the skin widen in a process known as vasodilation (*pictured right*). This results in transferral of more blood into the dermal regions. Some of this heat is then lost directly to the atmosphere in a process known as radiation.

4. **Conduction.** This is the transfer of heat from the body to cooler water or, if the horse is lying down, the ground. The cooler the water, the more effectively conduction removes heat.

Solar radiation

Evaporation of sweat

Contrating Muscles

Respiratory heat loss

BODY CORE

Contrating Muscles

Direct radiation and convection

Direct conduction

Ground thermo radiation

Reflected Solar radiation

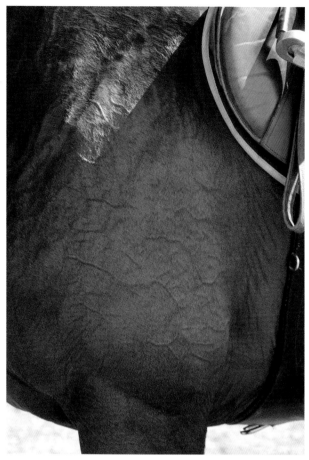

Vasodilation

Conversely the horse keeps warm by:

- **Insulation**. The horse makes use of the subcutaneous fat in the hypodermis
- **Vasoconstriction**. The capillaries under the skin contract to reduce heat loss through the skin
- **Shivering**. Rapid contraction of the muscles under the skin produces heat

The hair also has an important part to play in **temperature regulation**. In winter the horse adapts to the cold by growing a longer, thicker coat. In cold conditions, erector muscles pull the hair upright, trapping an insulating layer of air.

The Importance of Electrolytes

Horses and humans are the only animals that sweat through the skin. Horses sweat 3–4 times more than humans. Body fluid balance is finely controlled by electrolytes, which manage the movement of water into and out of cells. When lost in sweat, dehydration or overheating, fatigue, muscle problems and poor intestinal tract movement can occur. The major electrolytes are sodium, chloride, potassium, calcium and magnesium. It is important that these are replenished as soon as possible after exercise.

THE HOOF

The External Hoof

At the hoof, the skin cells modify into tubules filled with keratin. The external hoof is a horny extension of the epidermis growing downwards from the coronary band. It is thicker at the toe than the heel, takes up to 12 months to grow from the band to the toe, and consists of 25% water, which is drawn from both body fluids and the external environment. The hoof wall is covered with a thin layer of epidermis known as the periople, which is responsible for balancing the moisture of the hoof. The external hoof has neither blood supply nor nerves. This is the reason why shoes can be nailed on!

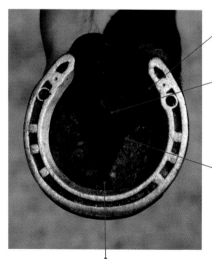

The bars – ridges formed as the heel turns inward

The insensitive frog – a wedge of soft, elastic horn with a central groove consisting of 45% moisture

The grooves – on either side of the frog

The sole – a plate of hard horn approximately 2cm thick, made up of 30% water, which flakes away in a natural shedding process

The main hoof functions are to:

- protect the underlying structures
- assist in weight bearing
- absorb concussion
- ensure healthy circulation. Blood flows down the leg into the digital cushion. The horse's weight compresses the frog and squeezes the blood out of the digital cushion. This helps it to circulate around the foot and lower leg.

The Internal Hoof

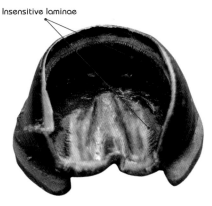

Insensitive laminae

Six hundred insensitive laminae growing outwards from the wall interweave with 250 sensitive laminae which grow outwards from the pedal bone, thus joining the hoof to the skeleton. This arrangement gives a large surface area that carries blood to all the components of the hoof and helps to distribute the weight. The white line, visible on the underside of the hoof, shows the junction between the sensitive and insensitive laminae. Laminitis, inflammation of the laminae, can result in the extremely painful separation of the sensitive and insensitive laminae.

Hoof Condition

The main factors influencing hoof condition are ensuring that the horse is in good physical condition and has a balanced diet. Hoof condition, growth and repair are dependant on nutrients from the blood and moisture levels. Hoof oils and conditioners only have a cosmetic effect. If the horse has a crack in the hoof wall or sustains an injury to the hoof, the only way it will repair is from the coronary band downwards at a rate of about 1cm per month. Changes in feed or condition can directly affect hoof health which can be seen as a ring in the hoof wall. Ideally healthy hooves should be dense and tough but not brittle. A hoof which has cracks and flakes away can be an indicator of poor health or a diet lacking in the correct vitamins and minerals. A good hoof supplement for hoof growth, repair and quality will contain biotin, sulphur, methionine, tryptophan choline, magnesium and zinc, although, if the horse is fed a nutritionally balanced diet, a supplement should not be necessary.

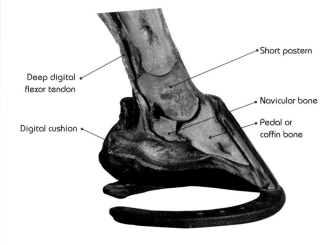

Short pastern

Deep digital flexor tendon

Navicular bone

Pedal or coffin bone

Digital cushion

There are two bones completely enclosed within the hoof capsule. The crescent shaped pedal or coffin bone, which is dense, light, porous and perforated with tiny holes to allow the passage of blood vessels and nerves and, the navicular bone which strengthens the coffin joint as the foot hits the ground. Together with the distal end of the short pastern these bones join to form the coffin joint, the main function of which is to absorb concussion and assist circulation. Several tendons and ligaments run down from the leg and attach to the bones within the foot. Beneath the coffin bone lies the digital cushion, a fibrous pad which contains a network of blood vessels.

THE SKIN AS AN INDICATOR OF HEALTH

The skin can provide insight into nutritional condition, the internal balance of body chemistry, the health of the internal organs and the horse's ability to resist infection. It should feel elastic, smooth, clean and slightly warm. Tight skin is an indicator of dehydration or poor diet. To test for dehydration pinch the skin. It should return to normal straight away.

Horses that live out should have a natural layer of protective grease which helps them overcome wet, cold conditions. This should not be removed by over grooming or bathing.

Unexplained sweating or evidence of dried sweat may indicate that the horse has been in pain from colic or may have a fever.

Obvious signs of skin problems are heat, pain, swelling, bruising, blistering, hives, ulcers, abscesses or scabs. These may be due to a variety of causes, which include:

- Injury caused by ill-fitting tack or rugs
- Bacterial, as in mud fever
- Fungal, as in ringworm
- Viral, as in warts
- Parasites, for example lice
- Exposure to noxious substances
- Allergy, as in urticaria.

An unhealthy, dull, or flaking coat lacking in sebaceous secretions can be an indicator of poor health, a diet lacking in nutritional balance, worm infestation or severe emotional stress.

Practical Application

- Groom regularly to remove dead cells and scurf to allow the skin to successfully perform its functions. This is particularly important in horses that are rugged or stabled. Meticulous attention should be given to the fetlocks and the dock.
- Feed a well-balanced diet. Fatty acids, particularly omega 3 and 6 found in lush green grass, linseed or sunflower oil, are an important nutrient group for the skin and coat. A diet too low in fat can be detrimental to health. (See page 66 – The Digestive System).
- Expose the horse's skin to the sunlight to allow synthesis of vitamin D. This is essential for the healthy growth of teeth and bones. Stabled horses may need a vitamin D supplement.

- Washing with shampoo removes the natural grease that builds up within the coat, critical for warmth. Removal of grease also leaves the skin susceptible to infection, bacteria, rain, grazes and sores. Avoid washing with shampoo if the horse is living out.
- Only use a non-biological washing powder for rugs and numnahs.
- To avoid dehydration and replace chemicals lost through sweat, feed electrolytes after strenuous exercise.
- Sweating effectively helps to detoxify and clean the skin and coat. This is why the coat is left feeling soft and silky after the sweat has been washed off following hard work.

The Skeletal System

The skeletal system provides a strong framework that supports the body, protects the muscles and vital organs and facilitates movement.

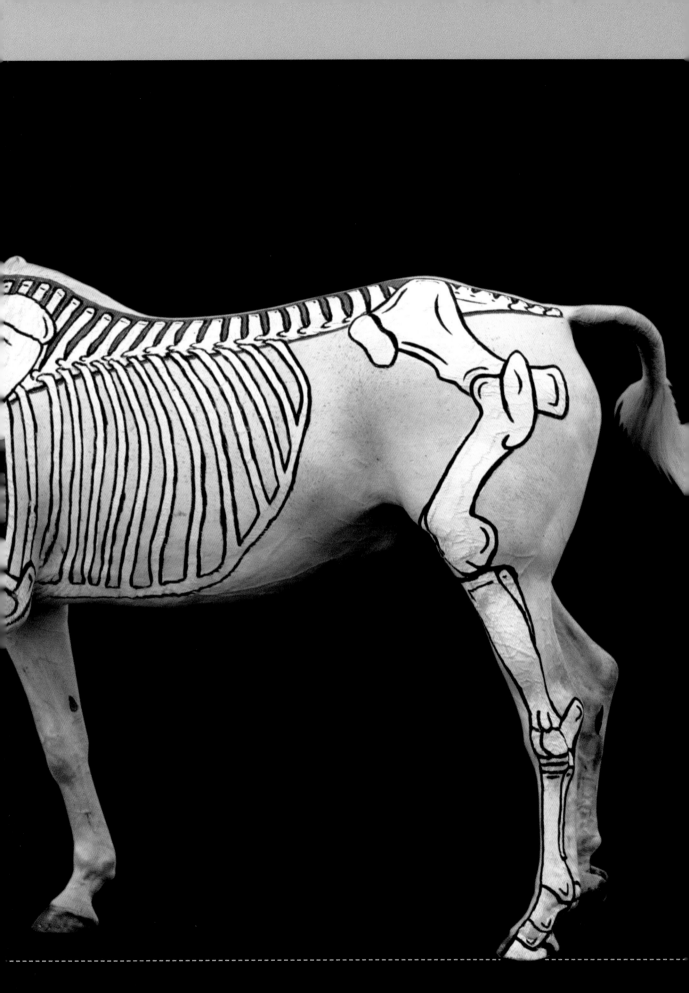

BONE

Bone is made up of calcium, phosphorus, sodium, other minerals and the protein collagen. It contains three types of cells: **osteoclasts**, which break down old or damaged bone, **osteocytes**, which carry nutrients and waste products to and from blood vessels in the bone, and **osteoblasts**, which repair damage and build up new bone. This continuous process is called bone remodelling and occurs in response to exercise.

As living tissue supplied with food and oxygen from the blood, bone is very responsive to changes in blood supply, nutrition, pressure and physical demand. It continually dies and grows and has the ability to lay down more layers for strength when required.

Bone consists of a dense, ivory coloured outer shell known as compact bone. About 80% of skeletal mass is compact bone. Small holes and channels carry blood vessels from the outer coating called the periosteum to the cancellous bone. Cancellous bone represents the spongy interior, which is filled with red marrow, responsible for the production of red and white blood cells and found mainly at the ends of bones, and yellow marrow, which is mainly fat and can be used as a last resort energy source in times of starvation.

Bones can be classified as:
- **Long bones** such as the radius, humerus and cannon bones. These are the main levers of the body that allow movement.
- **Short bones** such as the carpus and tarsus, which are strong, compact and act as shock absorbers within the joint.
- **Flat bones** found in the skull and scapular. These provide protection for the delicate organs beneath.
- **Irregular bones** which include the vertebrae and have projections for muscle and tendon attachment.
- **Sesamoid bones** such as the small bones within the fetlock that give strength and are found where a tendon passes over a joint.

Bones meet at joints, many of which are lined by cartilage or synovial fluid which helps reduce friction. The main movement joints are either hinge or ball and socket. They are operated by tendons which link muscle to bone and are supported by ligaments which link bone to bone (see page 58).

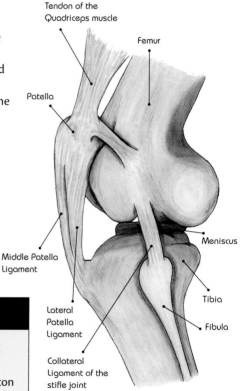

Cancellous or spongy bone

Compact Bone

Periosteum

Tendon of the Quadriceps muscle

Femur

Patella

Meniscus

Middle Patella Ligament

Tibia

Lateral Patella Ligament

Fibula

Collateral Ligament of the stifle joint

The patella is a type of sesamoid bone within the stifle which is the largest but weakest joint within the horse. The patella is held in place by three patella ligaments. It is part of the stay apparatus which 'locks' to allow the horse to sleep with minimum muscular effort. (See page 26)

The Skeleton

The skeleton consists of approximately 205 bones. This number varies as some bones fuse together as the horse matures. It can be divided into the Axial Skeleton made up of the skull, vertebrae and ribs, and the Appendicular Skeleton comprised the limbs.

The main function of the skeleton is to:

- support and provide a stable framework
- protect the internal organs
- provide attachment for muscles and tendons
- determine conformation, maintains posture and assists in movement
- produce and store red blood cells
- provide storage for fats and minerals – particularly important for mares in foal.

THE AXIAL SKELETON: THE SKULL

The skull consists of 34 flat and irregular bones connected by fibrous joints that ossify with age. It has 4 cavities – the **cranium,** which houses and protects the brain, the **orbital cavity** that surrounds and protects the eye and the **oral and the nasal cavities** which lead to the respiratory and digestive tracts.

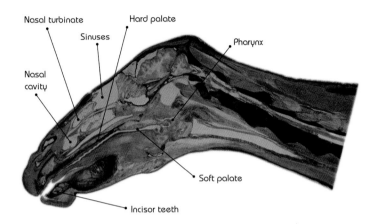

The nasal cavity is separated from the mouth by the hard palate. The soft palate separates the mouth and the pharynx. Behind the nasal cavity are the sinuses, which are large air spaces that secrete mucous and help to keep the skull light.

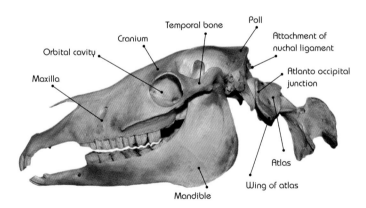

The skull attaches to the spine at the atlas forming the **atlanto-occipital junction**. The wings of the atlas, which provide an important area for muscle attachment, can be felt just below the poll. The poll is the highest point of the skull and the place most likely to be damaged by the headcollar if the horse pulls back. It is also vulnerable if he rears or hits his head in a confined space. A good reason to fit a protective cap when travelling!

The Teeth

The Teeth are inserted into the **maxilla** (upper jaw) and the **mandible** (lower jaw). The mandible attaches to the skull just below the base of each ear at the temporal bone creating the **temporomandibular joint** (TMJ). The function of the TMJ is to allow the mouth to open and close and to facilitate chewing in an elliptical type movement. Located close to the centre of balance, it plays an important part in the correct functioning of the muscular skeletal system. Any damage, degeneration, muscular tension or misalignment in this joint can adversely affect balance and movement.

Horses' teeth erupt throughout their lifetime in order to compensate for wear brought about by extended periods of chewing on tough plant material. Indeed, in the wild they constantly feed on a variety of vegetation for up to 18 hours a day. With the head down, teeth will wear evenly and the jaw will be aligned correctly. Today's horses are often stabled for long periods spending less time chewing and more with their heads up (see page 69). This affects how the teeth wear and often causes hooks and ramps which can result in cheek lesions. This in turn can affect concentration, head carriage and the movement of the TMJ. Any pain in the mouth or the TMJ may inhibit performance, athletic ability, physiological and emotional balance and has been cited as one possible cause of headshaking.

Practical Application

- Allow the horse to graze as much as possible and always feed from the floor. This minimises the risk of cranial and TMJ dysfunction.
- Signs of temporomandibular discomfort may include muscle asymmetry, heat or pain in the mandibular region and changes in the range of mandibular movement. Discomfort is often accompanied by observable changes in eating patterns, head carriage, performance, acceptance of the bit, clamping the jaw shut, grinding the teeth or trying to force the mouth open against the noseband.
- Horses chew predominantly on either the right or left side. This may affect ridden contact.
- Have the teeth regularly checked by a professional registered equine dental technician.

The Skeletal System

THE AXIAL SKELETON: THE SPINE

The spine consists of between 54 and 58 vertebrae separated by 185 fibro-cartilaginous and synovial joints that contribute to weight bearing, shock absorption and spinal flexibility.

The main functions of the spine are to:
- protect the spinal cord, the main route for nervous messages, which carry sensory and motor signals around the body (see page 113)
- provide areas for muscle and ligament attachment
- protect the main aorta which lies just below the vertebral bodies
- protect internal organs such as the kidneys which are situated close to the underside of the spine
- provide strength for the suspension of the torso

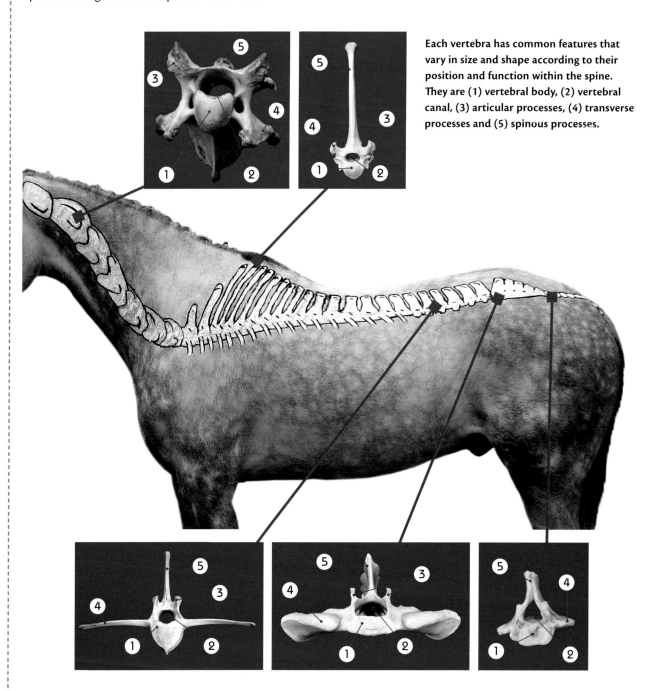

Each vertebra has common features that vary in size and shape according to their position and function within the spine. They are (1) vertebral body, (2) vertebral canal, (3) articular processes, (4) transverse processes and (5) spinous processes.

Cervical Vertebrae

The 7 neck vertebrae make up the most flexible section of the spine. They are arranged in an 'S' shape and sit much lower in the neck than is often realised. The cervical vertebrae also protect the oesophagus, trachea, main cervical nerves and blood vessels.

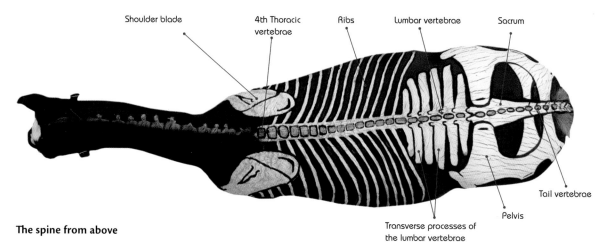

Shoulder blade | 4th Thoracic vertebrae | Ribs | Lumbar vertebrae | Sacrum | Tail vertebrae | Pelvis | Transverse processes of the lumbar vertebrae

The spine from above

Thoracic Vertebrae

The thoracic region is comparatively rigid and inflexible. This is due to the shape of the interconnecting articular processes and strong fibro-cartilaginous joints that restrict movement. It is the strength and rigidity of the spine in this area that allows us to ride our horses. The spinous processes of the thoracic vertebrae are longest at the withers. These provide bony attachment areas and leverage for the muscles, acting as a fulcrum for the nuchal and supraspinous ligaments which influence the positioning of the head and neck (see page 64). 18 pairs of ribs attach to the 18 thoracic vertebrae via synovial joints. The ribs provide protection for the heart, lungs, liver, stomach and much of the digestive system. They are flexible to allow for expansion and contraction with inhalation and expiration of breath. They also contribute to bend by coming closer together on the inside and further apart on the outside of the bend.

Lumbar Vertebrae

The lumbar region is composed of 6 vertebrae, which are flatter, wider and heavier than those in the thoracic region. This is the least flexible area of the back. The large, horizontal transverse processes provide extensive areas for muscle attachment offering strength and stability. Any power produced in the horse's hind end is transmitted forward to the rest of the body through the 6 lumbar vertebrae. Lateral movement is progressively restricted in the caudal direction. The lumbar region is supported by neither the pelvis nor the ribs making this area prone to muscle soreness and strain.

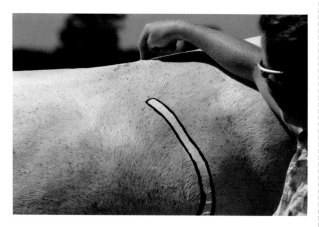

It is important that the saddle should not sit further back than the last thoracic vertebra. To find this point, feel for the last rib, follow it up until it disappears under the back musculature and from there, run your finger vertically up to the spine.

The Back

The thoracic and lumbar vertebrae together make up the back or **thoracolumbar** section of the spine. The interlocking vertebrae of the spine, bound together by cartilage, tendons, ligaments and muscular tissue, can be compared in construction to a suspension bridge. If any component becomes weakened or damaged, extra strain is put on other areas of the back, which can result in dysfunction. The thoracolumbar section of the spine is rigid to suspend the weight of the contents of the abdominal cavity.

The Skeletal System

Sacral Vertebrae

The 5 fused sacral vertebrae form the **sacrum.** This functions as one bone. The first sacral vertebra has an extended transverse process known as the sacral wing, which binds the pelvis to the spine via the wing of the ilium.

The Lumbar-Sacral Junction

The joint between the lumbar and sacral vertebrae is called the **Lumbar-Sacral Junction (LSJ)**. This is a hinge joint which can be felt at the point where the spinous processes of the lumbar vertebra slope forwards and those of the sacrum point backwards.

Lumbar vertebra

Lumbo-sacral junction

Sacrum

It is the LSJ that allows the pelvis to tilt and has a significant role to play in allowing the hind legs under the body when the horse canters, jumps or performs high level dressage movements. Although 20 degrees of flexion and extension at the lumbar sacral junction is possible, this degree of movement is not generally achieved. Rather like ourselves, we are all capable of, but only a few can actually do, the splits!

The greatest degree of flexion is usually seen in the sliding western halt.

The horse uses approximately 8 degrees of movement at the LSJ in a medium canter.

After the neck and tail, the LSJ is longitudinally the most flexible point in the spine. This area is the point at which the massive forces generated by both the muscles and bones of the hind limbs are absorbed and transferred forward along the back. At high speeds, when jumping or on hard ground, it is also where the concussive forces from the hind end meet the shock waves generated by the forelimbs as they hit the ground.

Maintaining stability and flexibility in this joint is the key for achieving collection, performing advanced dressage movements, successful jumping and allowing the horse to excel in any athletic event. Any restriction in movement here will be detrimental to the way the horse moves and affect how well he can engage from behind.

Pain from improper saddle fit, an imbalanced rider, stress or muscular tension in this vulnerable area can cause the back muscles to seize up, lose flexibility, restrict movement and impair performance. It is equivalent to us attempting to play sport with a painful lower back. Regular massage therapy, passive and active stretching together with careful progressive warm up is immensely helpful in maintaining flexibility throughout the muscles of the back and the LSJ.

Tail Vertebrae

Although the spinal cord and the main spinal ligaments peter out after the sacrum, a few do remain to allow the horse to carry and swish his tail. The posture of the tail is influenced by bundles of muscle fibres which surround the caudal vertebra. The contribution of the tail to movement is negligible but a change in the position can be an indicator of health further forward in the spine.

Tail movement and position

The tail is used for communication and contributes to body language. For example, agitated tail swishing indicates either psychological or physical discomfort. When the head is raised in excitement so is the tail. A dejected horse will stand with the head and tail both down. It is also thought a clamped tail indicates discomfort in the abdomen. Horses in season will hold their tail high and to the side particularly if there is a stallion in the vicinity. Stallions will indicate their interest in a mare by raising their tail. Rapid raising and lowering of the tail 'flagging' is often looked for by stud managers to confirm that ejaculation has occurred.

The Skeletal System

SPINAL FLEXIBILITY AND BEND

It is the rigidity of the back and the interlocking configuration of the vertebrae that allows the horse to support the heavy hindgut and carry the weight of the rider. Optimising the small amount of back movement, while maintaining strength and stability, is key to keeping the horse supple, improving performance and reducing the risk of tension and strain within his back muscles.

The spine bends in two ways:

1 Longitudinal Bend

This is either spinal flexion or extension. Flexion involves the horse lifting and rounding his back, and it occurs when he works either in a long and low outline or is correctly 'through' and 'on the bit'. Spinal extension, the opposite of flexion, occurs when the horse hollows his back and raises his head and tail. This posture is commonly associated with tension and the fight-flight response.

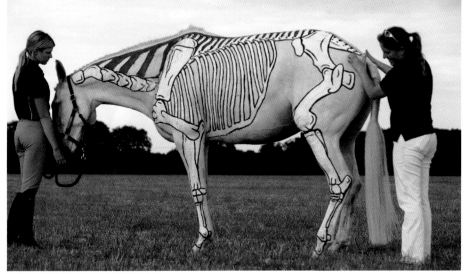

Spinal flexion

Longitudinal suppleness is required for the horse to have the flexibility and range of movement to perform engagement exercises in dressage, jumping and western riding movements, such as the sliding western halt.

Spinal extension

2 Lateral Bend

The horse does not bend evenly from poll to tail. Most lateral or sideways flexibility occurs within the neck and tail with only one to two degrees of bend occurring within the joints of the lumbar and thoracic vertebrae. The majority of this takes place in the caudal thoracic region right underneath the back of the saddle. The ribs also contribute to lateral flexibility by coming closer together on the inside of the bend and further apart on the outside. This gives the feeling of the horse 'bending' around the inside leg. The horse uses bend through his back and ribs when performing small circles or lateral work.

Within the horse's spine, the most inflexible part will not bend until the most flexible part has reached its end range of movement. Where the neck is taken only to the mid range of lateral movement (*above*), very little bend occurs in the mid spine region. Where the horse is really reaching around for the carrot, taking the neck towards its end range of lateral movement (*right*), some bend can be seen in the thoracolumbar vertebrae. Note the movement of the ribs in these photographs.

THE APPENDICULAR SKELETON: THE FORELIMB

At rest, the forelimb supports 60–65% of the horse's weight. This increases with force and speed. When landing from a jump of 1.10 metres for example, this rises to two and a half times his body weight.

Attachment to the Spine

The forelimbs are connected to the spine by the thoracic sling, a powerful group of muscles, tendons and fascia (see page 46) which significantly disperses and reduces the amount of concussion reaching the spine. As the forelimbs carry more weight, they are subjected to more concussion than the hind limbs.

Bones and Joints of the Forelimb

The **Scapula**, a large bone that glides over the first 7 ribs, has a large, flat surface area for the attachment of the muscles and ligaments of the thoracic sling. The top of the scapula is a semi-circular cartilaginous extension which feels and acts like bone. To ensure the scapula can move freely, it is important that at least two fingers can be inserted between it and the point of tree.

The scapula meets with the **humerus**, one of the strongest bones in the body, at the shoulder joint. This is a ball and socket joint, although the range of movement is curtailed by the fact the shoulder joint is encapsulated within the body.

A wider angle at the shoulder with a more upright scapula results in a reduced range of movement, a short choppy stride and a more uncomfortable ride. The angle of the shoulder and slope of the scapula is a useful conformational indicator of performance and an important consideration when examining a horse for purchase.

The **humerus, radius and ulna** make up the **elbow**, a hinged joint that can only move in one plane. An extension to the ulna, known as the **olecranon process**, provides an extended area for muscle attachment, allows greater leverage and makes extension of the shoulder and movement of the forelimb more efficient.

From the elbow downwards, the forelimb forms a strong, vertical column designed to carry weight and act as a prop. The heavy body is propelled over the prop by the forces created in the hind limb. Although the joints below the shoulder are hinge joints, there is a very small amount of passive lateral and rotational movement available to help the horse to cope with uneven ground.

The **knee**, equivalent to our wrist, consists of a series of hinged synovial joints linking 8 **carpal bones** arranged in two rows, which allows for effective absorption of concussion.

Below the knee are the cannon bone, two splint bones and the bones of the digital structures.

The **splint** bones are attached to the **cannon** bone by fragile ligaments. Their function is to add structural strength to the cannon bone and support the load through the knee. They are particularly susceptible to mechanical injury through being knocked by the other forelimb. The firm rounded lump commonly referred to as a 'splint' is caused by inflammation between the periosteum and the bone. While a splint is forming, it may be accompanied by pain, swelling and lameness. However, the lump will reduce once the inflammation subsides, and once ossified, it will remain but is unlikely to cause further problems.

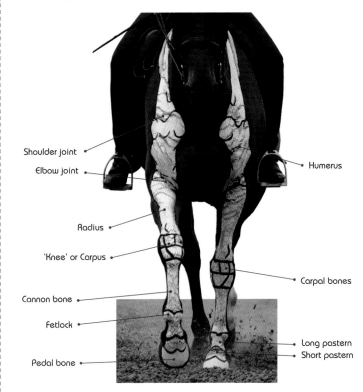

Shoulder joint
Elbow joint
Humerus
Radius
'Knee' or Carpus
Carpal bones
Cannon bone
Fetlock
Long pastern
Short pastern
Pedal bone

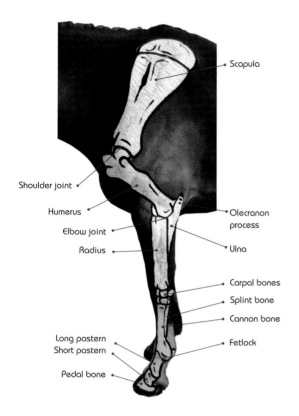

Scapula

Shoulder joint

Humerus

Elbow joint

Radius

Olecranon process

Ulna

Carpal bones

Splint bone

Cannon bone

Long pastern
Short pastern

Fetlock

Pedal bone

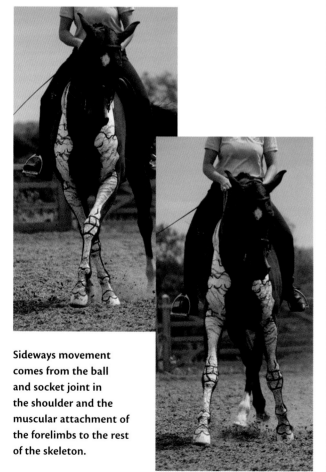

Sideways movement comes from the ball and socket joint in the shoulder and the muscular attachment of the forelimbs to the rest of the skeleton.

The **fetlock** is a hinge joint formed by the cannon bone, long pastern and two sesamoids bones. Sesamoid bones support the digital flexor tendons (see page 57) and create extra leverage for movement. It has flexion and extension, but minimal rotation. As the forelimb hits the ground, the elbow and knee are locked causing the fetlock to extend to absorb much of the concussion. As in all joints, the fetlock contains lubricating synovial fluid within a sac or capsule which prevents it leaking into the surrounding tissues.

The **long and** the **short pastern** are situated between the fetlock and the hoof. Ideally they follow the angle of the hoof wall, 40–45 degrees in the forelimbs and 50–55 degrees in the hind. The pasterns have limited movement but are vital in absorbing concussion. An upright pastern will bear direct weight and be more prone to concussive injury, whereas an over sloping pastern will put more strain on the tendons, ligaments and fetlock joint.

Windgalls

Windgalls are soft swellings found just above the fetlock when the tendon sheath becomes filled with synovial fluid. There are two types:

1. The more common **tendinous windgall**, which can come and go, is formed close to the skin. The lining of the tendon sheath between the suspensory ligament and the flexor tendon thickens, causing a soft  swelling to appear. They are often larger on the hind legs, and generally occur in older horses or those in hard work. There is rarely any associated pain or lameness.

2. The **articular windgall** is found in the fetlock of the fore or hind limb joint capsule between the suspensory ligament and the cannon bone. Articular windgalls generally show no sign of pain, heat or lameness, however, where pain and lameness are apparent, this can be a symptom of an underlying problem such as degenerative joint disease.

There are several causes of windgalls:
• concussion to the fetlock joint, which is thought to be the most common
• fetlock joint trauma
• heavy breed types or horses with short, upright pasterns are more susceptible.
The degree of swelling may vary according to the environmental temperature and exercise demand.

THE APPENDICULAR SKELETON: THE HINDLIMBS

Each hind leg carries about 20% of the horse's weight. The hind limb is the powerhouse of the horse. This is reflected in the large, strong bones which absorb and withstand the enormous forces created when pushing the body forward or upwards.

Attachment to the Spine

The hindlimb is attached to the spine by the pelvis at the **sacroiliac joint** (SIJ) The wing of the ilium attaches to the large transverse processes of the first sacral vertebra and is held securely in place by powerful ventral, dorsal and sacroiliac ligaments.

This is not a movement joint. It does not articulate like the hip or hock. Movement in this region actually comes from the LSJ (see page 22). The SIJ sustains a high loading force during athletic activity as it transfers power from the hindquarters through to the rest of the back.

The complexity of the region can be a source of back pain but the inaccessibility and depth of muscle mass makes problems difficult to diagnose. Outward signs of pain, whether attributable to the LSJ or the SIJ, include general stiffness, behavioural changes, lack of hind limb power, changing legs behind in canter, deterioration in quality of movement, reluctance to work from behind, round or lift the back, failure to perform flying changes or refusing to jump.

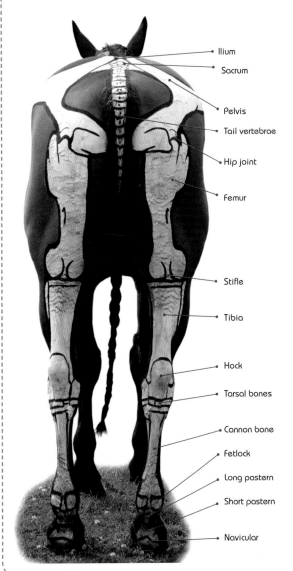

| Ilium |
| Sacrum |
| Pelvis |
| Tail vertebrae |
| Hip joint |
| Femur |
| Stifle |
| Tibia |
| Hock |
| Tarsal bones |
| Cannon bone |
| Fetlock |
| Long pastern |
| Short pastern |
| Navicular |

The pelvis is larger in the mare to allow for reproduction. It is the pelvis that determines the shape the hindquarters and the prominence of the 'jumper's bump'.

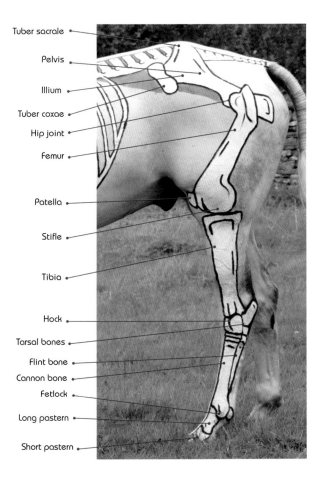

| Tuber sacrale |
| Pelvis |
| Illium |
| Tuber coxae |
| Hip joint |
| Femur |
| Patella |
| Stifle |
| Tibia |
| Hock |
| Tarsal bones |
| Flint bone |
| Cannon bone |
| Fetlock |
| Long pastern |
| Short pastern |

Bones and Joints of the Hind Limb

The **pelvis** consists of three fused bones:
1. The **illium** is the largest bone. The highest point, the **tuber sacrale,** forms the 'jumper's bump' whilst the outer edge, the **tuber coxae**, forms the false hip. This large bony protrusion can easily be felt and is often confused with the actual hip joint, which is much further back.
2. The **ischium** which forms the point of buttock.
3. The **pubis** which forms the pelvic floor and provides a large attachment area for the abdominal and pelvic floor muscles crutial for tilting the pelvis and lifting the back.

The leg bones join on to the pelvis at the hip where the ball shape at the top of the femur slots into the **acetabulum**, the cup formed at the junction of the three pelvic bones.

Although the hip is a ball and socket that does allow lateral movement, full rotation is restricted by the ligamental attachments and the location of the joint deep within the body.

Conformation

The alignment, lengths and angles of the bones determine conformation, balance and structural correctness. These are important indicators of athletic ability and long term soundness – particularly useful when examining a horse for purchase.

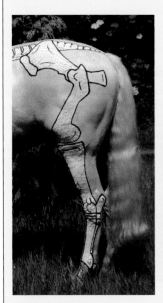
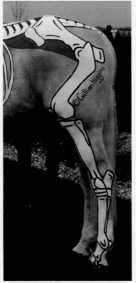

A horse with more obtuse hind limb angles will have reduced ability to step under, shorter stride length, reduced swing and spring, less smooth movement and be more prone to ligament strain and the detrimental effects of concussion.

More acute angles in the hind limb suggest greater potential for flexion, reach, spring, power, cadence and range of movement. Increased angulation also increases the absorption of concussion and provides a more comfortable ride.

During lateral exercises, the ability to step across the body comes from the hip joint. Movement in the joints from the stifle down is in a forward and backward plane, as these are hinge joints. As in the forelimb, there is some passive lateral and rotational movement to help the horse cope with uneven ground.

The **femur** is the strongest, heaviest long bone in the body. It angles forward and meets the **tibia** at the stifle. The **patella,** the equivalent to our knee cap, is located here (see page 18).

The **hock**, a multiple joint made up of 3 rows of **tarsal bones** and 4 joints, lies between the tibia, cannon bone and two splint bones. It behaves like a hinge joint and is equivalent to our ankle. The anatomy of the hock, together with the other joints in the hind limb, make it possible for the horse to accelerate, decelerate, turn sharply and propel himself upwards.

Below the cannon and splint bones, the fetlock, **sesamoids**, **long pastern**, **short pastern**, **navicular** and **pedal bone** have the same configuration as in the forelimb (see page 26 forelimb and page 13 hoof).

The Skeletal System

THE EFFECT OF EXERCISE ON THE SKELETON

Conditioning and Strengthening Bones

The skeletal system adapts to exercise, or lack of it, by forming or removing tissue. Throughout a lifetime, osteoclasts constantly remove old, and osteoblasts build new, bone. This remodelling, whereby bone changes its external shape and internal architecture in response to the forces placed upon it, is known as Wolf's Law and allows the skeleton to respond to the mechanical stresses of movement and training.

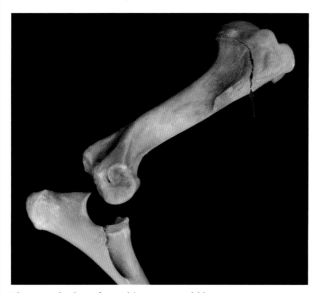

The growth plates from this two year old have not yet completely matured as the skeleton does not reach full maturity until the horse is between 4 and 6 years old. Excessive stress prior to maturation can result in skeletal damage.

Bone conditions much more slowly than other tissues and requires a low level of concussion to strengthen. Walking on the road, particularly with young or unfit horses, conditions bone without attracting injury.

Practical Application

• Plan an incremental training regime. As fitness progresses, short bursts of daily training at working trot or canter on a good to firm surface or working towards trotting on a hard surface for 10 minutes 3 or 4 times per week gives the bone time to strengthen, will effectively load the appendicular skeleton and will provide enough stimulus to elicit bone response.

• Horses working constantly on an all-weather surface can not increase bone density and are susceptible to concussion or injury when exposed to hard ground at competitions.

• Fast work for cardio-vascular fitness must be balanced with the requisites of slower conditioning of bone and the effects of concussion.

• Calcium and protein are essential for strong, healthy bones. Most complete feeds contain the correct balance and amount of nutrients.

Joint Movement

Taking joints through a full range of movement on a regular basis helps to maintain mobility and reduce the risk of repetitive strain injuries. Tendons will become thicker and able to withstand greater force and ligaments will stretch slightly to allow greater flexibility.

When a horse is on box rest, inactivity leads to insufficient production of synovial fluid, which causes joints to stiffen up. Passive mobilisations, which take the joint through a good range of movement, can help to stimulate joint fluid production.

Concussion

Concussion is the force sent up the leg each time it strikes the ground. It can cause stress, strain and even lameness. Concussion related problems include navicular disease, ringbone, sidebone, splints, micro-fractures as well as tendon and ligament strains.

Although force is absorbed by the foot, pastern, fetlock, knee, hock, shoulder and stifle, it is the strength of the bones in the legs which must bear the brunt of exercise and training. Excessive working on ground with no 'give', particularly at speed, together with incorrect conformation, magnifies concussion and exposes the horse to wear and tear on bones and joints.

Because horses carry more weight in front, concussion primarily affects the fore limbs. This is exacerbated by extra loading for example when riding or jumping downhill. On landing from a fence, the trailing forelimb absorbs most the impact which sends shock waves up the rigid bony column of the leg.

As well as putting strain on the heart and lungs, excess weight puts strain on the joints and magnifies concussion. Ideally the weight of the rider and tack should not exceed 20% of the weight of the horse.

The Skeletal System

Facts

- Bone needs to be strong to withstand the forces associated with mass, speed and gait.
- To increase bone density, exercise must be structured and progressive.
- It takes at least three years of appropriate training for bone to reach its maximum density.
- As bones become stronger, the hyaline cartilage at the end of bones becomes thicker to provide increased shock absorption.
- The entire musculoskeletal system continues to strengthen for up to 48 hours after the cessation of exercise. Beyond that time it will revert to its previous level. For effective conditioning, training needs to be sustained on a regular basis.
- The entire skeleton is replaced over a period of 7 to 10 years.
- As soon as a horse reaches skeletal maturity, the degenerative process begins.

COMPENSATION

Practical Application

Pushing unequally from behind may be due to discomfort or muscular weakness in one or both hind limbs. The horse may:
- find it easier to circle or perform lateral work on one rein
- jump to one side
- lose straightness
- have a preferred canter lead – often seen landing from a fence
- repeatedly rest the same hind leg in the stable
- have unequal muscle development over the hindquarters and back – particularly in the lumbar region
- have tight muscle on the strong side and weaker, more flexible muscles on the weaker side.

Exercises to encourage the horse to push equally include hill work, raised pole work and transitions on both reins.

If the horse pushes unequally from behind, the forces being transferred forward will also be unequal. This may result in compensatory movement patterns and secondary back pain. The arrows on the photograph indicate the possible flow of increased compensatory forces as a result of unequal pushing.

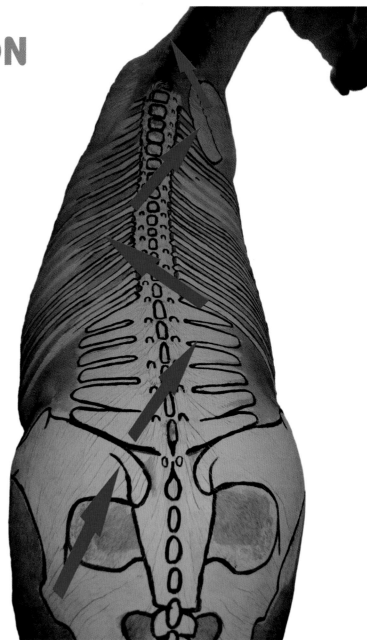

Strong bones, supple joints and correct conditioning are requisites of extreme dressage movements such as the levade.

SUMMARY

- Bones have to be strong to create, maintain and withstand the forces placed upon them.
- Bone can be remodelled in response to exercise and training.
- As part of the muscular skeletal system, the correct conditioning of bone is as important as that of muscles, ligaments and tendons.
- Unconditioned bones and associated structures are susceptible to strain, sprain and concussive injury.
- Regular varied exercise and plenty of turnout keeps bones strong and joints mobile and supple.
- Horses should be worked on a variety of surfaces.
- It is important to maintain a balance between working on a hard surface to condition bone and over working, which will induce concussion type injuries.
- As part of a training regime horses should be exposed to surfaces, gaits, speeds and conditions that simulate competition.
- Ensure the horse is regularly shod to allow the hoof to work correctly.

The muscular system

creates smooth,

flowing movement.

The Muscular System

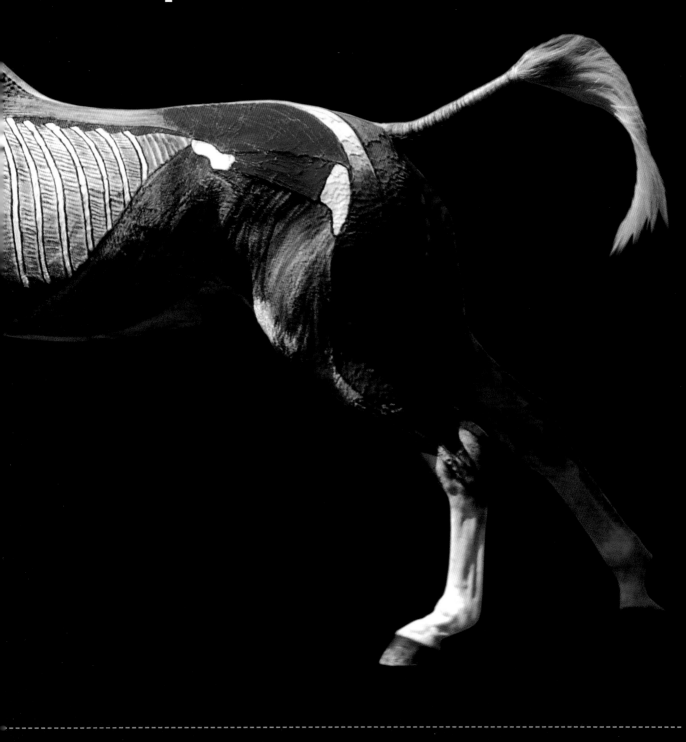

MUSCLES

Muscles control every aspect of movement, both internal and external. They form the largest tissue mass in the horse's body. There are various types of muscles performing a wide variety of tasks all working in a similar way. Electrical impulses instruct the fibres to contract and shorten then relax and lengthen.

There are 3 types of muscle. **Smooth** and **cardiac** which function automatically as a result of involuntary or autonomic activity within the brain, and **skeletal**, which, under voluntary or conscious control, co-ordinates and creates movement.

Smooth Muscle

This is involuntary muscle which functions automatically. It surrounds and is found in all internal tissues and organs. Smooth muscle responds to stimuli from the autonomic nervous system (see page 116). It is responsible for pushing food through the digestive system and for the physical control of bladder and bowel. It is also found in the vascular and reproductive systems.

Cardiac Muscle

This highly specialised, strong, thick and striated muscle is fatigue resistant. Beating around 100,000 times a day throughout the horse's lifetime, it co-ordinates the propulsion of blood in and out of the heart (see page 83).

Skeletal Muscle

There are more than 700 different skeletal muscles in the horse. **The brain sends a signal to the muscles via nerves which then convert chemical energy into movement and the muscles, which are highly elastic and have strong contractile powers, react accordingly.**

The function of skeletal muscle is to:
• support the skeleton and create movement
• maintain joint stability and posture
• control range of movement
• protect the skeleton and internal organs from trauma
• contribute to thermoregulation by shivering.

Fact

The muscles attach to the bone via the periosteum at the **point of origin**, which is nearest the body centre, and the **point of insertion**, which is furthest away.

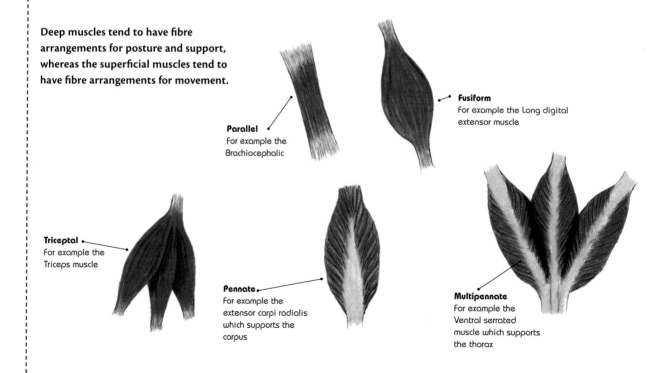

Deep muscles tend to have fibre arrangements for posture and support, whereas the superficial muscles tend to have fibre arrangements for movement.

Parallel
For example the Brachiocephalic

Fusiform
For example the Long digital extensor muscle

Triceptal
For example the Triceps muscle

Pennate
For example the extensor carpi radialis which supports the carpus

Multipennate
For example the Ventral serrated muscle which supports the thorax

DEEP MUSCLES

The function of the deep muscles is posture and stability. They:

• attach directly to the bone
• are located close to the joints
• often have a number of points of origin and insertion
• are often responsible for supporting individual joints for example, the deep gluteal muscle only affects the hip joint
• have a high number of nerve endings, which makes them more sensitive to postural alignment

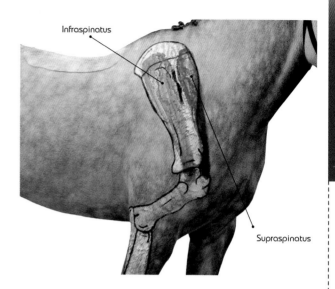

Infraspinatus

Supraspinatus

These deep muscles play a similar role to ligaments, stabilising the shoulder and reducing lateral movement.

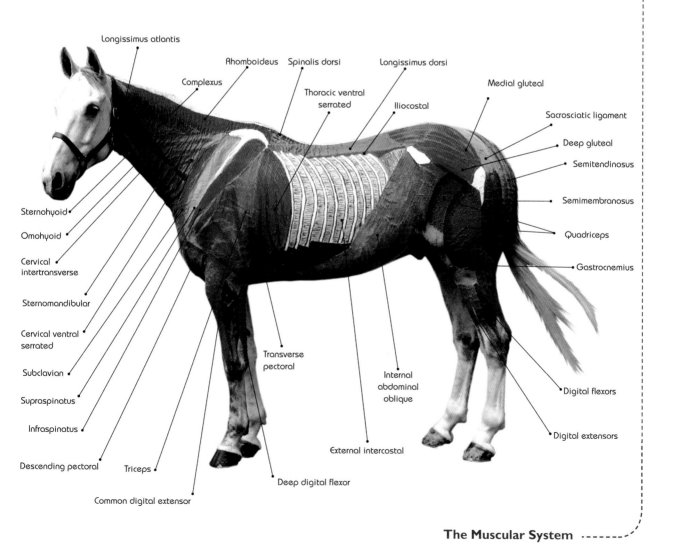

Longissimus atlantis

Rhomboideus Spinalis dorsi Longissimus dorsi

Complexus

Thoracic ventral serrated

Iliocostal

Medial gluteal

Sacrosciatic ligament

Deep gluteal

Semitendinosus

Semimembranosus

Quadriceps

Gastrocnemius

Sternohyoid

Omohyoid

Cervical intertransverse

Sternomandibular

Cervical ventral serrated

Subclavian

Supraspinatus

Infraspinatus

Descending pectoral

Triceps

Common digital extensor

Transverse pectoral

Deep digital flexor

External intercostal

Internal abdominal oblique

Digital flexors

Digital extensors

SUPERFICIAL MUSCLES

The superficial muscles are located between the deep muscles and skin. Although they vary in size and shape, they are generally classified as movement muscles. They are either:

- **bulky**, such as the superficial gluteal muscles, which are around 25cm thick in a 16hh horse, the triceps muscles, which are around 20cm thick, or the masseter muscle that moves the jaw or

- **sheet like**, such as the abdominal oblique muscles, which span the entire abdomen and contribute to rib movement, bend and protraction of the hind limb.

The surface of the superficial muscles can easily be felt for tension, heat and swelling. They are readily influenced by complementary therapies, such as massage, magnetic therapy, active and passive stretches.

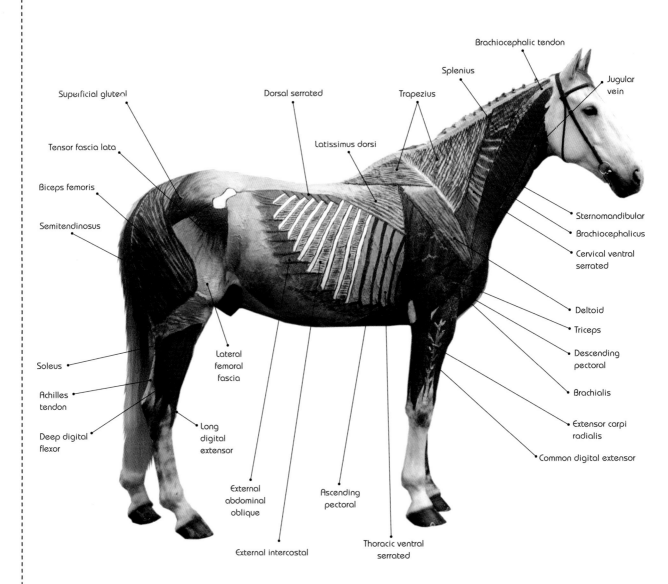

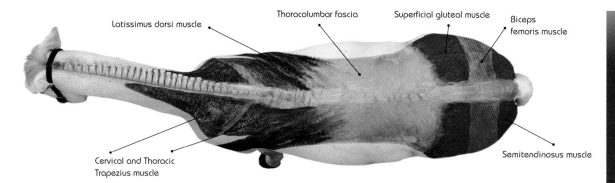

Superficial muscles are located further away from bone and joints, thereby having points of origin and insertion into fascia and other muscles as well as bone. The latissimus dorsi and superficial gluteal muscles attach into the thoracolumbar fascia.

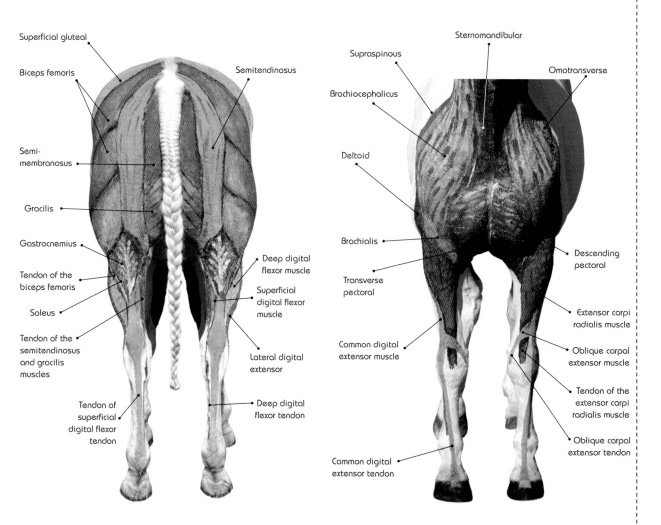

Superficial muscles in the hindquarters are large and powerful. Those running down the back of the hind legs extend the hip, stifle and hock joints and push the horse forwards over the planted hind limb.

Superficial muscles between the front legs support the thorax and attach the forelimbs to the rest of the body, whilst those running down the front of the forelimbs bring the leg forwards in protraction.

The Muscular System - - - - - - -

HOW MUSCLES CONTRACT

Muscles are made up of thousands of fascicles which are bundles of fibres running parallel to each other and bound together by thin layers of fascia. This is what gives muscle its striated appearance. Within each fibre are thousands of other smaller threads known as myofibrils.

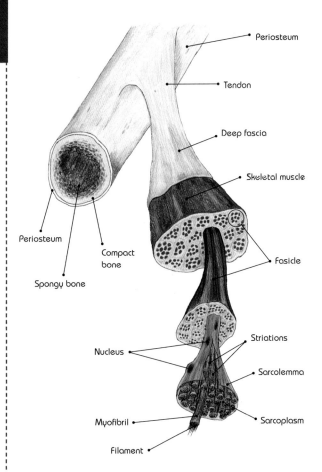

Within each myofibril are millions of minute bands known as sarcomeres, which are made up of two proteins, myosin and actin. When chemical messages are sent to the muscle via a nerve, smaller actin filaments slide between the larger myosin filaments causing it to shorten and contract.

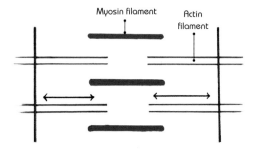

Muscle Fibres

There are two types of muscle fibres:

1. Slow twitch fibres work slowly for long periods of time. They are very red as they contain high levels of myoglobin, which stores and supplies oxygen for aerobic energy production.

2. Fast twitch muscle fibres are powerful and fast contracting. They are much lighter in colour as they contain less myoglobin than slow twitch. They can produce energy rapidly with anaerobic respiration, however they also tire more quickly.

Every horse has a mix of fast and slow twitch fibres. The proportions are determined by breed and genetics. Horses with a higher proportion of slow twitch fibres have more stamina, tire less easily and make good endurance or leisure horses. Those with a higher proportion of fast twitch fibres have less stamina but more explosive energy. They make good show jumpers. A three day event horse requires both aerobic stamina for dressage and cross-country and anaerobic capability for jumping effort. Appropriate training can bring each type of horse to its peak level of fitness but will not change the type of muscle that it has by birth. It is not possible to change a show cob into a steeplechaser! Despite limitations imposed by nature, training can enable each horse to use his muscular strength, power, speed, and endurance to reach his full potential.

Types of Muscle Contraction

There are two main types of muscle contraction:

1. Isometric contractions occur when the muscle is working statically to maintain a position. In the human this could be holding a heavy object in the hand at arm's length. After a time, the muscle would burn. In the horse this can equate to holding the weight of the head in a fixed outline.

2. Isotonic contractions result in movement and can be further divided into:
• **Concentric**, where the muscle shortens to create movement, such as when the horse is trotting or cantering.
• **Eccentric**, where the muscle controls the movement, for example when landing from a jump, braking, going downhill or coming to a sudden halt.

Horses use a combination of isotonic and isometric contractions. Dressage horses performing advanced movements, particularly those involved in exaggerated flexion of the joints in the hind limbs or when required to carry more weight on the hindquarters, use isometric and eccentric muscle contraction to maintain the posture.

Muscle Pairs

Movement is created by skeletal muscle applying force to bone via a tendon to operate a joint. Muscles work by contracting and relaxing in pairs. The muscles that contract are known as **agonists** whilst those that relax in opposition are known as **antagonists**.

Agonist muscle

Antagonist muscle

Motor signals via the brain instruct the triceps muscle running down the back of the forelimb to contract to extend the elbow. At the same time the biceps muscle running down the front of the shoulder and elbow relaxes.

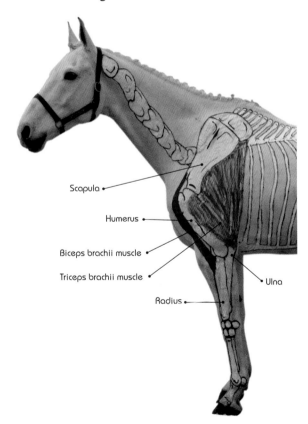

Scapula

Humerus

Biceps brachii muscle

Triceps brachii muscle

Ulna

Radius

The triceps and biceps are a good example of how muscles work together in pairs.

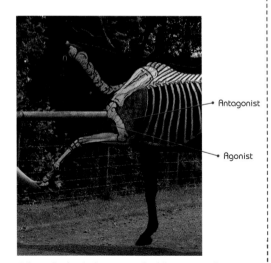

Antagonist

Agonist

When the brain instructs the biceps muscle to contract and the triceps to relax, this allows the elbow to flex.

MUSCLE CHAINS

As no body part is moved by one muscle alone, joints are operated by groups of pairs. These then combine into chains which co-ordinate to create smooth movement.

1. The Extensor and Flexor Chains

The large muscle chains that link the spine and hind limbs are responsible for creating forward movement.

The extensor and flexor chains combine to form a circle of muscles which allow the body to support the weight of the rider and gracefully orchestrate smooth, balanced movement and equilibrium. Pain or discomfort in any muscle along a chain can manifest itself elsewhere. For example, soreness in the lumbar region behind the saddle, a common site for tension, will affect other muscles in the chain and cause deterioration in suppleness, stride length and posture.

The Extensor Chain

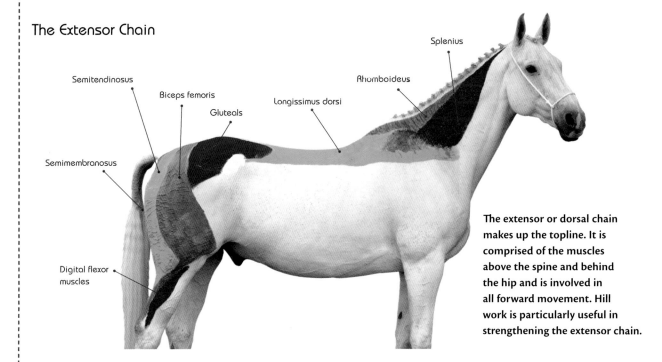

Semitendinosus

Biceps femoris

Gluteals

Semimembranosus

Longissimus dorsi

Rhomboideus

Splenius

Digital flexor muscles

The extensor or dorsal chain makes up the topline. It is comprised of the muscles above the spine and behind the hip and is involved in all forward movement. Hill work is particularly useful in strengthening the extensor chain.

Concentric contraction of the extensor chain muscles results in extension of the neck, back and hip joints. This is also seen when kicking, bucking and rearing!

The Flexor Chain

The flexor or ventral chain makes up the bottom line. These muscles lie underneath the spine, in front of the hip, and include the abdominal muscles. They form part of the 'core' muscles which are vital in supporting and maintaining correct posture of the back. Engagement exercises, for example half-halts and walking over raised poles, help to tone and strengthen the flexor chain of muscles.

Brachiocephalic

Sterno-mandibular

Tensor
fascia lata

Iliopsoas

Abdominal
muscles

Quadriceps

Digital flexor
muscles

Concentric contraction of the flexor chain muscles results in flexion of the neck, back and hip joints.

The Muscular System

2. Lateral Spinal Muscle Chains

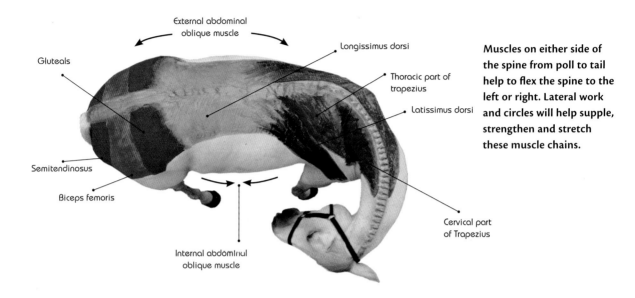

External abdominal oblique muscle

Gluteals

Longissimus dorsi

Thoracic part of trapezius

Latissimus dorsi

Semitendinosus

Biceps femoris

Cervical part of Trapezius

Internal abdominal oblique muscle

Muscles on either side of the spine from poll to tail help to flex the spine to the left or right. Lateral work and circles will help supple, strengthen and stretch these muscle chains.

3. Forelimb Muscle Chains

Muscles which run down the front of the leg (shown in orange and yellow) bring the leg forwards whilst those down the back (shown in blue and green), help pull the bodyweight over the planted limb during the stance phase. The exception to this rule is the trapezius muscle, which works as a fixator to stabilise the top of the scapula.

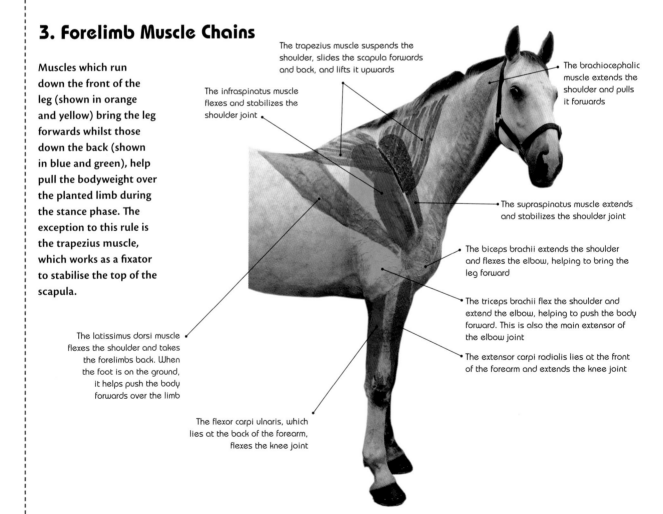

The trapezius muscle suspends the shoulder, slides the scapula forwards and back, and lifts it upwards

The infraspinatus muscle flexes and stabilizes the shoulder joint

The brachiocephalic muscle extends the shoulder and pulls it forwards

The supraspinatus muscle extends and stabilizes the shoulder joint

The biceps brachii extends the shoulder and flexes the elbow, helping to bring the leg forward

The triceps brachii flex the shoulder and extend the elbow, helping to push the body forward. This is also the main extensor of the elbow joint

The extensor carpi radialis lies at the front of the forearm and extends the knee joint

The latissimus dorsi muscle flexes the shoulder and takes the forelimbs back. When the foot is on the ground, it helps push the body forwards over the limb

The flexor carpi ulnaris, which lies at the back of the forearm, flexes the knee joint

CORE MUSCLES

Core stability provides the strength and co-ordination for control, balance, posture and carrying weight. It can improve self carriage, enhance performance and reduce the risk of injury. Core muscles include the thoracic sling, abdominal muscles, pelvic stabilisers and deep vertebral muscles. Ridden exercises to strengthen the core focus on engagement of the hindlimbs to lighten the forehand; these include frequent transitions and half halts encouraging the horse to collect and push from behind, hill work, and pole work using raised trot and canter poles.

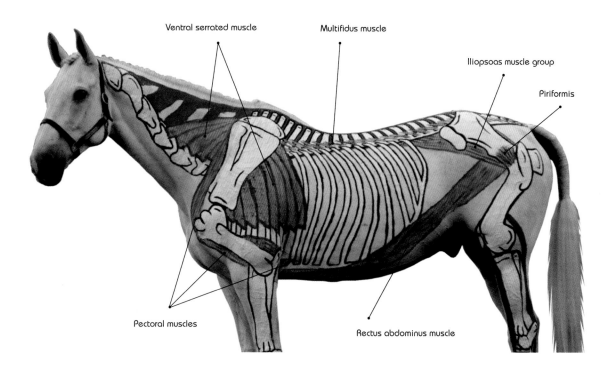

Ventral serrated muscle

Multifidus muscle

Iliopsoas muscle group

Piriformis

Pectoral muscles

Rectus abdominus muscle

In hand exercises to strengthen the core include carrot stretches, backing up, walking over raised poles and back lifts.

The Muscular System

Thoracic Sling Muscles

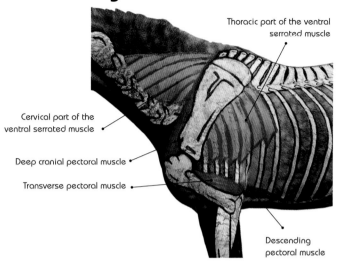

Thoracic part of the ventral serrated muscle

Cervical part of the ventral serrated muscle

Deep cranial pectoral muscle

Transverse pectoral muscle

Descending pectoral muscle

As the forelimb is not attached to the rest of the skeleton by bone, the thoracic sling muscles play an important role in supporting the forehand between the front legs.

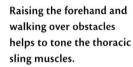

Raising the forehand and walking over obstacles helps to tone the thoracic sling muscles.

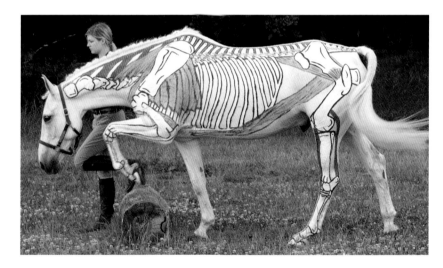

As the thoracic sling muscles contract, they lift and lighten the thorax between the forelimbs at the withers. As these muscles strengthen, the horse may appear to grow in height.

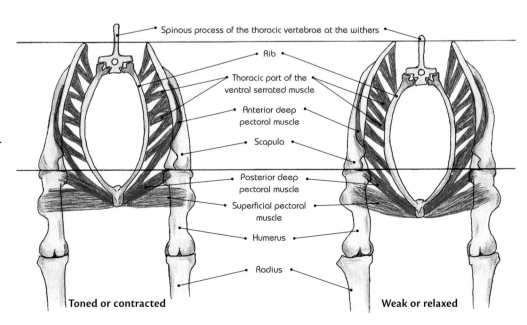

Spinous process of the thoracic vertebrae at the withers

Rib

Thoracic part of the ventral serrated muscle

Anterior deep pectoral muscle

Scapula

Posterior deep pectoral muscle

Superficial pectoral muscle

Humerus

Radius

Toned or contracted

Weak or relaxed

Abdominal Muscles

Weak abdominal muscles can result in poor back posture.

Toned abdominal muscles support the back.

Pelvic Stabiliser Muscles

The **Iliopsoas** muscle group supports and stabilises the underside of the lumbar sacral and pelvic regions. It maintains posture and creates flexion in the lumbar sacral junction and hip. The pelvic stabilisers also play an important role in supporting and stabilising the hindquarters. In dressage movements, where more weight is carried by the hindquarters, the iliopsoas works isometrically and eccentrically in a shortened frame. Dressage horses therefore are more prone to tension in this muscle group (see picture page 41).

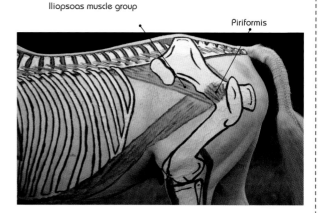

Iliopsoas muscle group

Piriformis

Deep Vertebral Muscles

The **multifidus**, the main muscle in this group, maintains individual vertebral posture and stability by attaching the base of each individual spinous process to the vertebral body. As it is highly innervated, the multifidus is very sensitive to any changes in the alignment of individual vertebrae. If back pain causes the multifidus to atrophy, its role will be assumed by the longissimus dorsi. As this is a movement rather than a stabilising muscle, this will compromise the integrity of the spine.

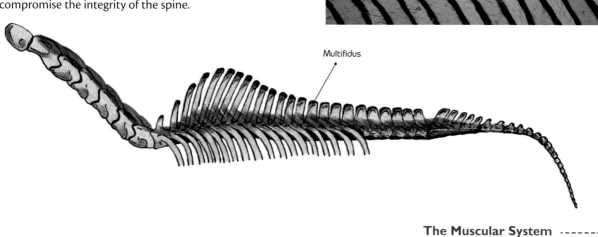

Multifidus

THE BENEFITS OF A WELL CONDITIONED MUSCULAR SYSTEM

How Muscles Adapt to Training

Muscle is the most adaptive tissue in the body. It adapts to training and contractions become more efficient by:

- increasing the number, size and type of muscle fibres
- increasing the number of capillaries within the muscles that increase blood flow and nutrients
- increasing the storage capacity of oxygen and efficient removal of waste
- increasing the number of mitochondria within the cells that provide the power for the muscle fibres to contract
- increasing the number and activity of muscle enzymes required for respiration
- increasing the ability to store glycogen
- improving aerobic and anaerobic respiration capacity which allows the horse to work longer and faster
- engaging in exercise which incorporates isometric, concentric and eccentric muscle contractions (see page 65/40).

This will lead to improved muscle co-ordination, strength, speed and endurance.

Strong, healthy and well- defined muscles enable the horse look good, feel good and perform with ease, accuracy and flair. This improves posture, power, balance and precision, makes the horse gallop faster, jump higher and sustain pace for longer, all with a reduced risk of injury.

Muscles Develop Slowly

A strong muscular system goes hand-in-hand with a well-conditioned cardiovascular system. One cannot be improved without the other. Conditioning muscles relies on a consistent, progressive, planned programme. Muscle changes occur slowly, taking 4–12 weeks depending upon age, breed, fitness and condition. Asking too much too soon in the form of speed, distance and carrying weight for long periods, results in fatigued, sore or damaged muscles which delays the conditioning programme and is counterproductive. Once established, muscle condition usually lasts for several weeks. Missing 1–2 weeks training due to minor injury does not affect overall muscular fitness in the same way as it does with human athletes.

Muscles must be trained for:

Endurance

Long, slow-distance work (LSD) using aerobic respiration develops muscular endurance which enables muscles to sustain performance at sub maximal levels. This is essential for all horses in all disciplines, especially for eventing and endurance horses. Time and distance must be extended gradually, moving on to the next stage only when current targets are met. This ensures progressive muscle loading without overtaxing a muscle. For a horse coming back into

work, 15 minutes a day walking is a good starting point. Then add 10 minutes a day gradually introducing trot and some canter work. The aim is to achieve 45 minutes of mixed gait work easily. It is important at this stage to condition all muscles equally to avoid putting strain on any particular part. LSD can take place out hacking or in an arena (see page 98). Correct nutrition in the form of a balanced, high-energy diet is essential in supporting the muscles and the prevention of muscle disorders (see chapter 8).

Strength

Muscular strength is important for stability, balance, posture, weight carrying capacity, control, accuracy of movement and performance. Strengthening exercises result in joint stability, improved muscle tone and an increase in the number of muscle fibres which increases muscle bulk, power and strength. Strength training should be part of a structured conditioning programme. In order to avoid fatigue and allow muscles time to recover, it is important not to perform strength training sessions more than 2 or 3 times per week.

General muscle strengthening is accomplished with short bursts of varied high-intensity exercises such as:
• **hill work**, including transitions, lateral work and rein back, both up and down hill
• **raised pole work**, progressively increasing the height at walk and trot
• **performing** half steps of piaffe and passage
• **gymnastic jumping**, including grids and related distances progressively widening and heightening the obstacles
• **working on a loose, deep surface**. This must be

approached gradually to reduce the risk of injury to muscles, tendons and ligaments
• **riding through water,** which encourages the horse to lift his legs, clear and make the muscles work harder through the effect of drag.

Following a general muscular fitness programme, **discipline specific movements** are the most effective form of muscle strength training.

Co-ordination

Muscles become unco-ordinated when fatigued.

Well co-ordinated muscles work consistently, efficiently and accurately, improve posture and physical performance and reduce the risk of soreness and injury; dressage movements become well orchestrated and jumping more accurate. Muscle co-ordination and recruitment patterns are improved by repetition. This forges neural pathways which improve muscle co-ordination and efficiency in an upward spiral. It is more productive to practise a new movement for 10 minutes every other day rather than for an hour once a week. Co-ordination can be improved by practising cross-country jumps, such as a series of steps, sunken roads, banks, offset rails and ditch-rail-ditch on a regular basis.

Suppleness

A supple horse, like a supple person, can move with ease, enjoy flexibility and a wide range of movement and be less prone to strain. This feel-good factor contributes to concentration, co-operation, trainability and 'joie de vivre'. A combination of strength, co-ordination and suppleness results in the horse moving with relaxation, rhythm, contact, impulsion, straightness, collection, balance and flexion. This enables him to demonstrate submission, cadence and throughness, necessary for well-executed dressage movements, accurate and flowing jumping and symmetrical muscle development.

Suppleness exercises which increase range of movement, athletic ability and technical skills can be enhanced by:
- taking the joints and muscles through a full range of movement on a regular basis
- spending 5–10 minutes performing suppling exercises for warm up and cool down. This is particularly important if focussing on strength training
- interspersing strength and fast work with flexibility sessions
- performing ridden active stretches
- varying head and neck positions using a forwards and down outline and lateral flexion
- lateral suppling work, such as leg-yield, shoulder-in and travers, incorporating varying degrees of angle and bend
- stretch work and flexibility exercises on the lunge
- agility work both ridden and in-hand, such as bending exercises and stepping over raised poles.

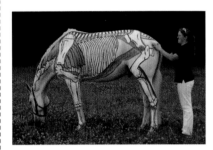

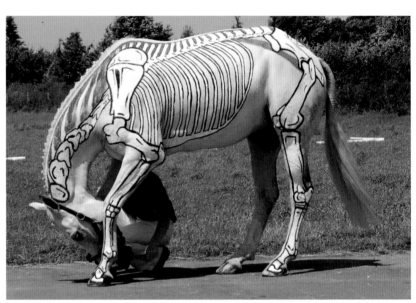

Performing a wide range of passive and active stretches will enhance suppleness.

Turning the horse out where he can constantly move, roll, bite flies, scratch and stretch will enhance suppleness. Stabled horses have less opportunity to move and can be more prone to stiffness.

Speed

Fast work increases the rate of muscular contractions, as well as co-ordination and mental reactions.

Once a horse can trot or canter easily for about an hour, including hill work, he is ready to start fast work. Once every 4 days is ideal, as this allows the stores of glycogen used in anaerobic exercise to be replenished. It also speeds up the rate of muscular contractions and increases the number of fast twitch fibre types. Begin by galloping for about 100 yards then gradually increase the distance returning to walk through canter and trot. This also allows the lactic acid produced as a by-product of anaerobic respiration to disperse. During fast work, about 20% of food is converted into energy. The rest is converted into heat and dissipated. Some heat improves muscle contractions. However, if the muscles overheat due to environmental conditions or the inability of the body to cool through evaporation or convection (see page 12), this will expose the muscles to fatigue, exhaustion and risk of injury.

Practical Application

- **Maintain a good posture** to encourage balance between the antagonistic muscle chains.
- **Train** for strength, endurance, suppleness, skill and speed.
- **Plan a structured programme.**
- **Vary work and include cross-training** to add variety and ensure all round suppleness, balance, rhythm and muscle development. This will avoid overuse of particular muscle groups and prevent repetitive strain type injuries.
- **Include athletic, event-specific training**.
- **Warm up** thoroughly to allow the muscles to be at the optimum temperature for performance (see page 60).
- **Cool down** slowly to reduce the risk of delayed onset of muscle soreness.
- **To promote the use of fast twitch fibres**, make sure all work is active and steps are marching – even just walking in from the field.
- **Include ridden, passive and active stretches**.
- **Regular massage** is an excellent way to monitor and maintain healthy muscles, as well as helping the muscles relax and reducing tension.
- **Allow plenty of time for rehabilitation, recovery and retraining** following muscle injury.
- **Feed enough protein** for essential amino acids which are important for muscle development and function (see page 71).
- **Keep tired muscles warm**.
- **Regular turnout** reduces the risk of muscle stiffness.
- **Daily walk work** is particularly important for stabled horses.

SUMMARY

- **Muscles control every aspect of internal and external movement.**
- **There are 3 types of muscle, smooth cardiac and skeletal.**
- **Muscles have both slow twitch and fast twitch fibres.**
- **Deep muscles tend to be responsible for posture and stability.**
- **Superficial muscles tend to be responsible for creating large gymnastic movements.**
- **Muscles of opposite action work together.**
- **Muscles groups are linked and work together as chains.**
- **Muscles must be conditioned slowly.**

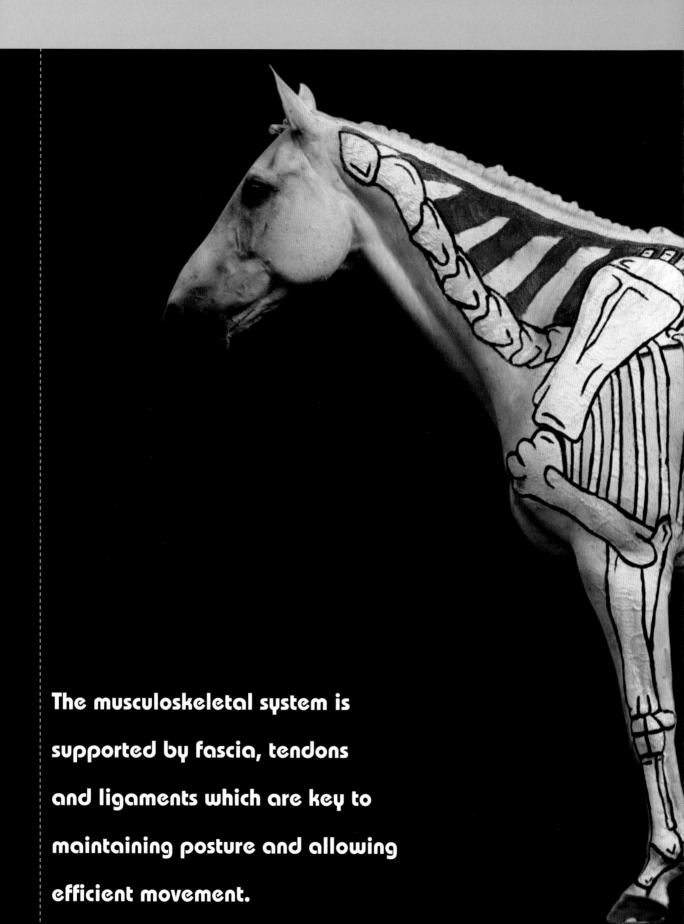

The musculoskeletal system is supported by fascia, tendons and ligaments which are key to maintaining posture and allowing efficient movement.

Fascia, Tendons and Ligaments

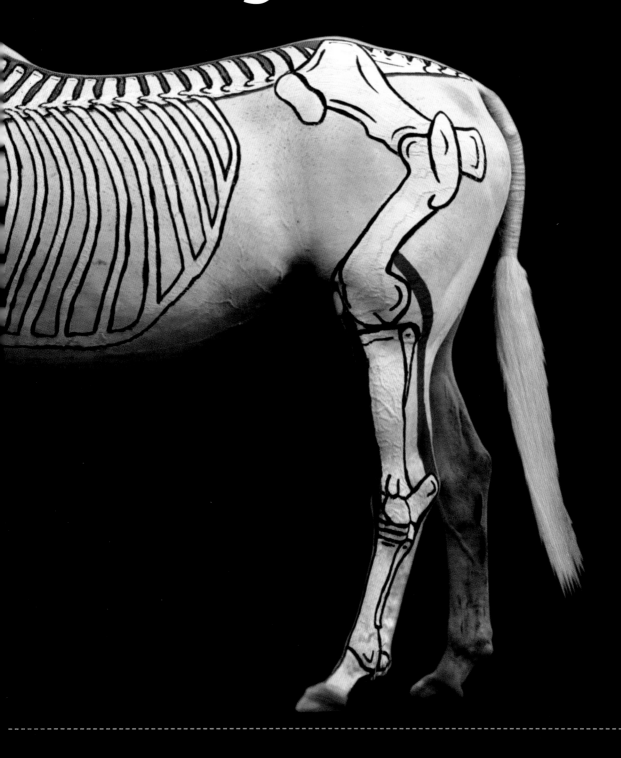

CONNECTIVE TISSUE

Connective tissue is found throughout the body. It makes up a number of physical structures including fascia, tendons, ligaments, cartilage, blood (see page 90), bone (see page 18), adipose (see page 149) and lymphatic tissue (see page 102). It is composed mainly of cells, fibres and collagen, a fibrous protein accounting for about 25% of the total protein content of the body. Much of the connective tissue is composed of different proportions of two main collagen fibre types:

1. White fibres which are relatively inelastic
2. Elastic or yellow fibres which have the capacity to stretch.

FASCIA

Fascia is an uninterrupted web of soft, dense, tissue that permeates, surrounds and intertwines with every muscle, bone and organ in the body, binding it together and allowing it to operate as one homogenous unit. It is the thin white glistening sheet-like material that can be seen when preparing to cook a chicken. It provides support, protection and an area for muscle attachment. It acts as a shock absorber for the muscles and assists movement by allowing them to slide against each other without interference. It is the high density of white collagenous fibres within the fascia that gives it strength and resilience. In its optimal condition, it is loose, moist and mobile.

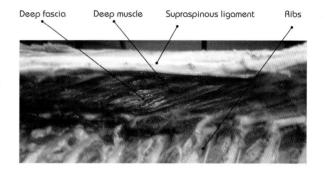

Deep fascia   Deep muscle   Supraspinous ligament   Ribs

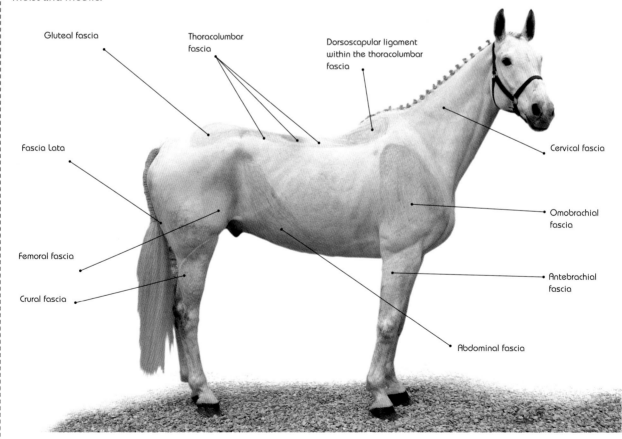

Gluteal fascia

Thoracolumbar fascia

Dorsoscapular ligament within the thoracolumbar fascia

Fascia Lata

Cervical fascia

Femoral fascia

Omobrachial fascia

Crural fascia

Antebrachial fascia

Abdominal fascia

Part four

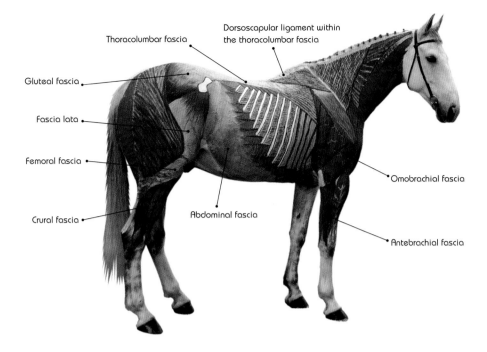

Fascia consists of several layers of overlapping, interwoven tissue named after their location.

Thoracolumbar fascia

Dorsoscapular ligament within the thoracolumbar fascia

Gluteal fascia

Fascia lata

Femoral fascia

Crural fascia

Abdominal fascia

Omobrachial fascia

Antebrachial fascia

Superficial Fascia

The superficial part of the fascia binds the skin to the muscles and underlying structures providing a pathway for nerves, lymph and blood vessels to enter the muscles. It also serves as an insulating layer reducing heat loss and cushioning the muscles from physical trauma.

Deep Fascia

Deep fascia is dense, irregular connective tissue that penetrates, surrounds and envelops the muscles, ligaments, tendons, joint capsules, periosteum, bones, nerves and blood vessels. Each layer of muscle is wrapped in a thin, sheath of fascia until it reaches its required bulk. The muscle fibres then reduce, narrowing in circumference and continuing as tendons.

Faulty Fascia!

When damaged or strained the fascia becomes less pliant and slightly tight, rather like wearing restrictive clothing which can inhibit movement. Because of its continual nature and close interrelationship with muscles, when one part is damaged, it can affect structures in a different part of the muscle chain (see page 42) far removed from the original site of injury and presenting seemingly unrelated symptoms such as stiffness or reduced range of movement.

Practical Application

- The condition of superficial fascia can be influenced by various massage techniques, passive and active stretching and myofascial release.
- Dehydration has a negative affect on fascia.

The Superficial Structures of the Back from Above

Musculature in the lumbar region, where the gluteal muscles and powerful hip and lumbar-sacral extensors which push the horse forwards, transfer their force through to the back via the thoracolumbar fascia.

Raising the forehand in dressage, jumping, hillwork and even bucking or rearing, all put the thoracolumbar fascia under further stress, making it one of the most common places for soreness and tension.

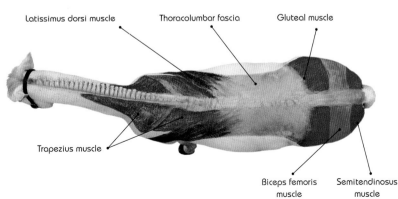

Latissimus dorsi muscle

Thoracolumbar fascia

Gluteal muscle

Trapezius muscle

Biceps femoris muscle

Semitendinosus muscle

TENDONS

Tendons are fibrous cords of connective tissue that connect muscle to bone. They are found throughout the body but generally it is the tendons of the lower leg which are of more interest when considering anatomy for performance.

- Tendons are formed when the muscle bulk tapers into dense, longitudinally arranged, parallel bundles of collagen which have high tensile strength allowing them to withstand enormous loads.
- The fibres within tendons are arranged in a slightly zig-zag or crimped pattern, which allows them to stretch and recoil by approximately 4%. Beyond this, damage will occur.
- Each tendon inserts into the periosteum via small spikes known as 'Sharpey's fibres'.
- New collagen is produced from cells called fibroblasts, which are interspersed between the collagen fibres.
- Old collagen is constantly being replaced by new fibres. The entire tendon is replaced every 6 months.
- Where a tendon crosses a joint it is protected by a synovial sheath and supported by an annular ligament.
- As there are no blood capillaries within the tendons, poor blood supply makes them slow to heal.

Healthy tendons are well defined and feel firm. Tendons in younger horses appear to be more robust than those in more mature horses.

Tendons of the Lower Leg

The horse has no muscles below the knee or hock. This makes the limbs lighter and enables the horse to move faster and more efficiently. As movement in the joints from the elbow and stifle down is only in the forwards and backwards plane, the tendons in the lower leg are either extensors or flexors.

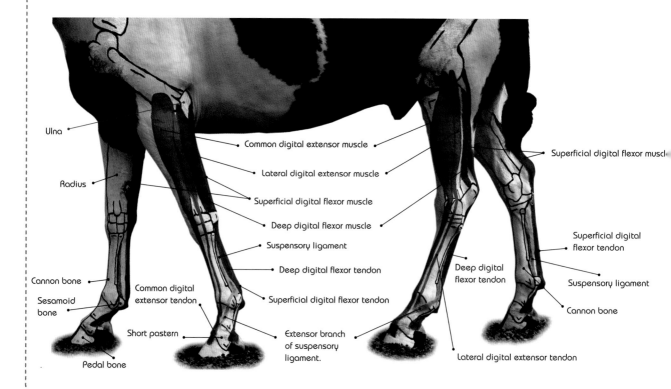

Ulna

Common digital extensor muscle

Superficial digital flexor musc[...]

Lateral digital extensor muscle

Radius

Superficial digital flexor muscle

Deep digital flexor muscle

Superficial digital flexor tendon

Suspensory ligament

Deep digital flexor tendon

Deep digital flexor tendon

Suspensory ligament

Cannon bone

Common digital extensor tendon

Sesamoid bone

Superficial digital flexor tendon

Cannon bone

Short pastern

Extensor branch of suspensory ligament.

Lateral digital extensor tendon

Pedal bone

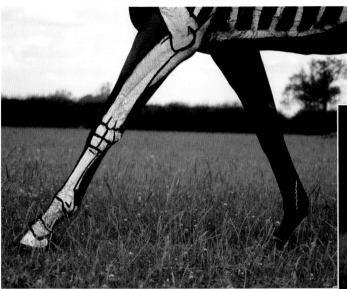

The digital extensor muscles and tendons come into play during the latter part of the swing phase of the stride. They help to position the hoof ready for impact and weight bearing.

The digital flexor muscles and tendons operate whenever the horse picks up and flexes his fetlock and pastern joints for example when jumping and during the first part of the swing phase in walk. By using elastic recoil during the faster paces, tendons save energy and create movement without the parent muscle having to work as hard (see page 59).

Fascia, Tendons and Ligaments

LIGAMENTS

Ligaments are fibrous bands of tough connective tissue that connect bone to bone. They control range of movement and are found throughout the body including the spine, pelvis, hip, stifle and limbs.

- Ligaments stabilise, protect, support and prevent joints from over extending, over flexing or over rotating.
- Ligaments are formed from strands of collagen that criss cross and overlap. This makes them stronger and less elastic than tendons. Like tendons they are susceptible to injury and when they do become strained their limited blood supply makes them slow to heal.
- If ligaments are overstretched or injured, the joint becomes weaker as the elongated ligaments are unable to properly support it.

There are four different types of ligament:

- Those that **support or suspend** a joint. For example, all limb joints are protected by collateral ligaments that limit lateral and rotational movement
- **Annular**, which wrap around the joint. These consist of broad bands of connective tissue that direct the pull on a tendon. An example is the annular ligament of the fetlock joint
- **Inter-osseus**, which link adjoining bone, for example the interspinous ligament between the spinous processes of the vertebrae and the sacrosciatic ligament of the pelvis
- **Funicular**, for example the funicular part of the nuchal ligament (see page 63).

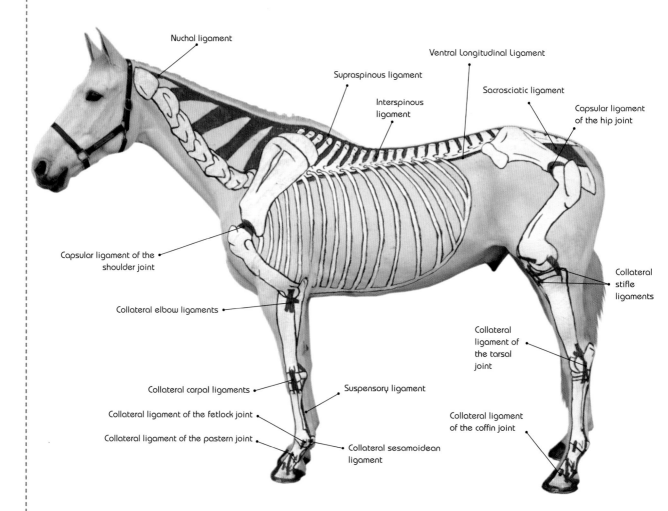

Ligaments are composed of mainly white inelastic collagenous fibres with a lesser variable content of slightly more elastic yellow fibres. The proportion of yellow fibres determines the amount of 'stretch' in a ligament. Capsular ligaments in ball and socket joints such as the hip, have a larger proportion of elastic yellow fibres to allow for range of movement.

THE SUSPENSORY LIGAMENT

The role of the suspensory ligament, which runs down the back of the lower leg, is to support and stabilise the fetlock. Although it is made up predominately of collagen fibres there are some residual muscle fibres. These, together with its higher proportion of yellow fibres, give the ligament its ability to stretch.

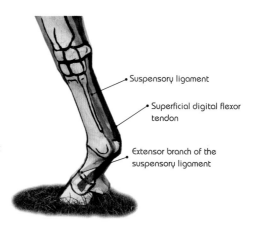

Suspensory ligament

Superficial digital flexor tendon

Extensor branch of the suspensory ligament

Due to their high elastic fibre content, the suspensory ligament and the superficial digital flexor tendon (SDFT) work closely together as a muscle energy saving mechanism particularly at faster speeds when carrying more weight or jumping.

Stretch and Recoil of the Fetlock Suspension System – An Energy Saving Mechanism

Stretch...

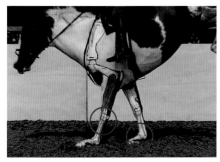

...and Recoil

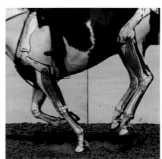

Most weight is taken on the trailing forelimb as this lands first and is perpendicular to the ground.

When landing from a fence, the suspensory ligament and the SDFT stretch to absorb upwards of 2½ times the horse's weight.

As the body rolls over the planted limb, the fetlock joint extends putting enormous strain on the fetlock suspension system. At this moment there is hyper-extension of the fetlock and carpal joints (see red circles).

Just like a taught elastic band, when pressure is released from the suspensory ligament and the SDFT, they spring back to their original length. This helps to pull the fetlock joint back towards a flexed position.

As the forelimbs snap up they are almost instantaneously replaced by the hind feet.

Tendon Injury

Performance horses that gallop or jump are most at risk of tendon injury. Over extension, particularly on a regular basis, can result in strain to the flexor tendons. Severe damage or rupture of the suspensory ligament may occur suddenly or over time. With dressage horses, the hind limb suspensory ligaments are particularly vulnerable to repetitive strain injuries.

Stretch

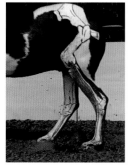

Release

Recoil

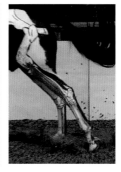

(*left*) **The suspensory ligament and the superficial digital flexor tendon play the same stretch and recoil role in the hind leg.**

Fascia, Tendons and Ligaments

TENDON AND LIGAMENT INJURIES

Tendon and ligament strains, sprains and tears are common in the lower leg of performance horses.

- Repetitive strain, the most common training related injury, can result in progressive degeneration.
- Factors which may lead to damage are: overworking a tired horse, direct trauma, damage to the parent muscle, poor conformation such as long sloping pasterns, poor hoof balance, carrying too much weight, rough, deep or hard ground and excessive fast work too early in training before the horse is conditioned.
- Injuries are most common in flexor tendons, check ligaments and the suspensory ligament.
- Inflammatory changes associated with the tearing of collagen fibres produce heat, swelling, pain and reduced function – although not all need to be present. In the case of mild strain there is little or no heat, pain or swelling.
- If injury is gradual rather than acute, it is known as tendonitis. The term for inflammation of the suspensory ligament is desmitis.
- If tendon or ligament damage is suspected, the vet must be called immediately. Swift action influences long term recovery.
- Prompt application of cold therapy and pressure bandaging is essential to control inflammation. Application of ice to the limb will constrict ruptured blood vessels and slow bleeding and bruising.

A bowed tendon occurs with tendonitis of the SDFT.

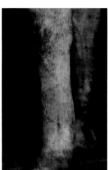

Using cryotherapy in the form of standing in running water or the sea, cool boots, spa, ice or cold hosing a few hours after fast work helps reduce inflammation.

Why Tendon and Ligament Injuries are Slow to Heal

Tendon and ligament injuries may take 12–18 months to heal. The healing process follows 3 stages which cannot be hurried:
1. Damaged tissue is removed by phagocytes (white blood cells). Collagen has a poor blood supply so the process is slow particularly in the mid cannon bone area.
2. Fibroblasts migrate to the area to produce new collagen.
3. Scar, or granulation tissue is then remodelled.

Repaired scar tissue is not as elastic as original collagen due to its haphazard non-parallel organisation. This is an important factor when assessing the prognosis for a successful return to competition. New techniques incorporating stem cell therapy are now emerging to promote re-growth of healthily organised tendon rather than scar tissue.

Avoiding Injury

- As their elastic limit is doubled when warm, tendons are less prone to injury if warmed up gradually. Cold tendons are less pliable and more susceptible to damage.
- Excessive heat generated by protective leg gear when riding at speed can weaken the collagen fibres. If not removed immediately after exercise, retained heat can increase tendon temperatures to 46–47°C. Tendons are more susceptible to injury when they have a high core temperature.

To maintain optimum tendon health:
- use well-ventilated boots that allow efficient. convection cooling of the lower legs during exercise.
- remove boots and actively cool the legs as soon as it is safe to do so after fast work.
- avoid using bandages for a prolonged period of time or if the horse is engaged in fast work. Bandages increase the heat within the structures more than boots, increasing the time it takes to cool the legs.
- ensure protective and support bandages are firm but not tight, and include the fetlock.
- feel legs every day to detect early signs of heat or swelling.

THE STAY APPARATUS

The stay apparatus is a unique system of interlocking muscles, tendons and ligaments that allow the joints in the limbs to be 'locked' and body weight to be suspended with little muscular effort. This arrangement allows the horse to sleep standing up. The muscles, tendons and ligaments of the stay apparatus also have an important role in movement.

The Forelimb Stay Apparatus

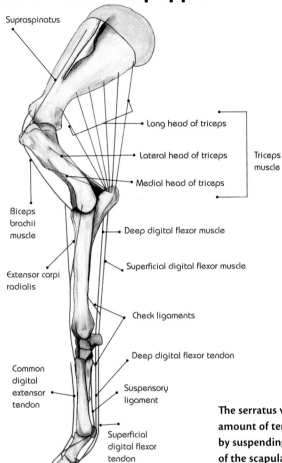

Supraspinatus

Long head of triceps

Lateral head of triceps · Triceps muscle

Medial head of triceps

Biceps brachii muscle

Deep digital flexor muscle

Superficial digital flexor muscle

Extensor carpi radialis

Check ligaments

Deep digital flexor tendon

Common digital extensor tendon

Suspensory ligament

Superficial digital flexor tendon

The Biceps Catapult

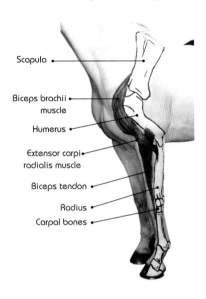

Scapula

Biceps brachii muscle

Humerus

Extensor carpi radialis muscle

Biceps tendon

Radius

Carpal bones

The powerful biceps brachii muscle and tendon and the extensor carpi radialis muscle, important parts of the stay apparatus, work together to support the shoulder and elbow.

The serratus ventralis muscle, which contains a large amount of tendinous tissue, supports the stay apparatus by suspending the weight of the torso from the underside of the scapula.

Stretch ... (Stance phase)

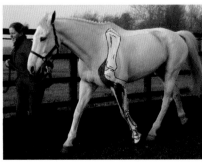

Horses engaged in repetitive fast work such as racehorses, are prone to tendonitis of the biceps tendons.

When the elbow and shoulder extend to reach their end range of movement, the biceps brachii muscle and its tendon is put under tension.

... and Spring Back (Swing phase)

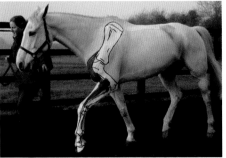

As the weight is transferred to the opposite limb, tension is released and the leg springs forward. This catapult action reduces the muscular effort required to pull the leg forward.

Fascia, Tendons and Ligaments

The Hind Limb Stay Apparatus

The Locking Mechanism of the Stifle

The stifle is locked by the quadriceps muscle lifting and rotating the patella then hooking it with the patellar ligament over a protuberance on the femur (see page 29). Locking is complete when most of the weight is on one limb with the other leg resting on the toe with one hip sagging lower than the other. This can be quickly reversed by unhooking the patellar ligament thus releasing the stifle. When resting, the horse can often be seen transferring his weight from one hind leg to the other.

The Reciprocal System

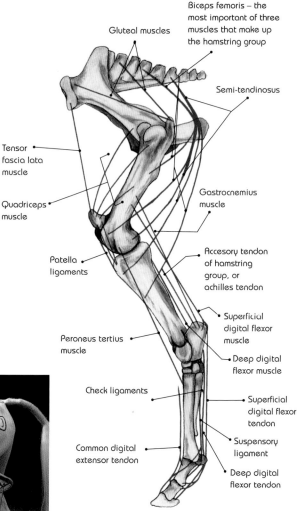

Biceps femoris – the most important of three muscles that make up the hamstring group

Gluteal muscles

Semi-tendinosus

Tensor fascia lata muscle

Quadriceps muscle

Gastrocnemius muscle

Patella ligaments

Accesory tendon of hamstring group, or achilles tendon

Peroneus tertius muscle

Superficial digital flexor muscle

Deep digital flexor muscle

Check ligaments

Superficial digital flexor tendon

Common digital extensor tendon

Suspensory ligament

Deep digital flexor tendon

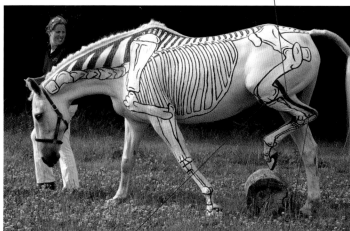

Superficial digital flexor muscle

Peroneus tertius muscle

Same amount of flexion

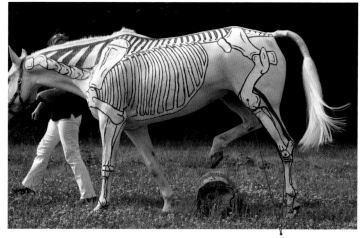

Same amount of extension

In the hind limb the peroneus tertius and the superficial digital flexor muscles, which have a high proportion of white collagenous fibres, operate as ligaments rather than muscles. Lack of stretch means the angles between the femur and tibia at the stifle and between the tibia and cannon bone at the hock are always the same. This causes the hock and stifle to work in tandem. This is known as the reciprocal system. It can also be seen in the levade (see page 33).

SPINAL LIGAMENTS

The **nuchal ligament** is one of the most important structures in the horse's body. It has two parts:
1. The **funicular** or cord like part which consists of two chords of strong fibrous material that run from the occipital bone to the withers.
2. The **lamellar** or sheet like part which descends from the funicular cord to the tops of the cervical vertebrae below.

The nuchal ligament continues as the **supraspinous ligament** which links the top of each spinous process from the withers to the end of the sacrum. The **intraspinous ligament** fills in the spaces between the spinous processes stabilising the spine. The **ventral longitudinal ligament** runs beneath the spine linking all the vertebral bodies. These 4 ligaments 'wrap' the vertebral bodies in a cocoon of strong, ligamental material that strengthens, stabilises and protects the spine.

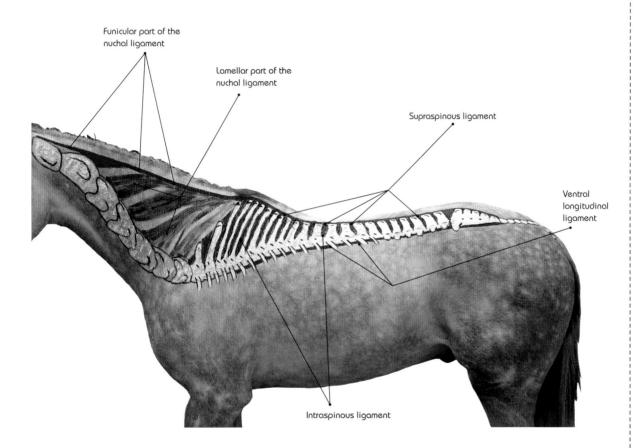

Funicular part of the nuchal ligament

Lamellar part of the nuchal ligament

Supraspinous ligament

Ventral longitudinal ligament

Intraspinous ligament

The Importance of the Nuchal Ligament

This energy saving device reduces the amount of muscular effort required to support, raise and lower the heavy head, hold it in position and maintain correct alignment of the cervical vertebrae. When a horse is dozing his head is suspended by the nuchal ligament. Its high proportion of yellow fibres makes it more elastic than other ligaments allowing it to stretch when the horse is ridden in an outline.

How Positioning the Head and Neck Affects the Back

The nuchal ligament restrains and stabilises the movement of the spinous processes at the highest point of the withers. This acts as a fulcrum which together with the supraspinous ligament supports the positioning of the back. The nuchal and supraspinous ligaments have an important role to play in maintaining spinal posture.

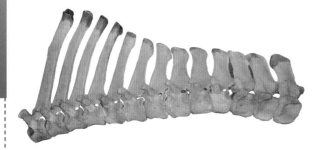

The thoraco-lumbar region of the spine should be straight or curved slightly upwards. This maintains correct posture and enables the back to fulfil its role in carrying weight, co-ordination, movement and balance.

If the vertebral bodies curve downwards this may result in the spinal processes becoming nearer together as well as putting pressure on the nerves and soft tissues of the spine. Poor posture can be the root of many muscular, ligamentary, osteoarthritic and movement problems within the back.

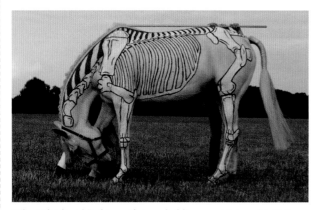

When the head is down, the nuchal ligament is taught. This pulls on the supraspinous ligament, which attaches to the spinous processes of the thoracic vertebrae at the withers, prising them slightly apart, causing the back to rise and the ribcage to lift.

It is important for young, weak or tired horses to stretch forwards and down. This enables them to use the relationship between the nuchal and supraspinous ligaments to support the back, carry the weight of the rider and maintain correct posture.

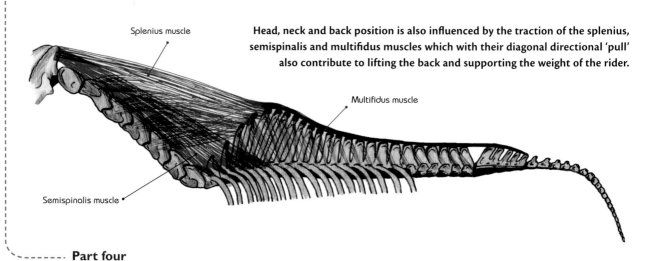

Splenius muscle

Head, neck and back position is also influenced by the traction of the splenius, semispinalis and multifidus muscles which with their diagonal directional 'pull' also contribute to lifting the back and supporting the weight of the rider.

Multifidus muscle

Semispinalis muscle

As the horse comes into a more advanced outline and the poll becomes the highest point, the role of the nuchal ligament diminishes as the muscles are required to work progressively harder for increasing lengths of time. During training, particularly if the horse starts to fidget, it is important to return to a forward and down neck outline for frequent breaks. This allows the nuchal ligament to take the strain and the muscles to relax and recuperate.

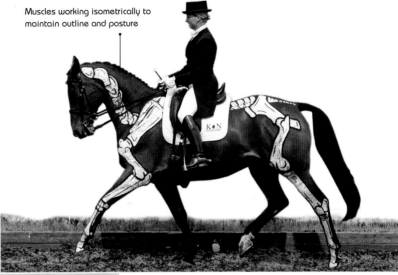
Muscles working isometrically to maintain outline and posture

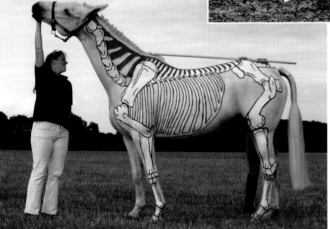
When the head is raised, the nuchal ligament slackens and the neck hollows. The resulting lack of tension in the supraspinous ligament causes the unsupported back to hollow. Horses that habitually go in a hollow outline are more prone to back problems.

Practical Application
- **Feeding** from the floor is essential for correct back posture. Feeding from a high haynet puts the back under continual strain as well as compromising the respiratory system (see page 69).
- It is important to give the horse space to get his head down when **travelling**. Holding the head in a high unnatural position, often for many hours, forces the horse to use isometric muscle contraction to maintain balance. This can lead to soreness, stiffness and muscle problems.

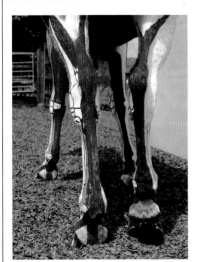

SUMMARY
- Fascia, tendons and ligaments are composed of connective tissue.
- Damage to fascia can affect range of movement.
- Tendons connect muscle to bone and are involved in movement.
- Ligaments connect bone to bone and control a joint.
- Most injuries to the tendons, ligaments or fascia are as a result of repetitive strain.
- Tendons and ligaments in the lower limb have a poor blood supply which makes them slow to heal.
- The flexor tendons and suspensory ligament are most at risk of injury.
- Exercise increases the strength of tendons and ligaments.
- Positioning of the head and neck can affect back posture.

The Digestive System

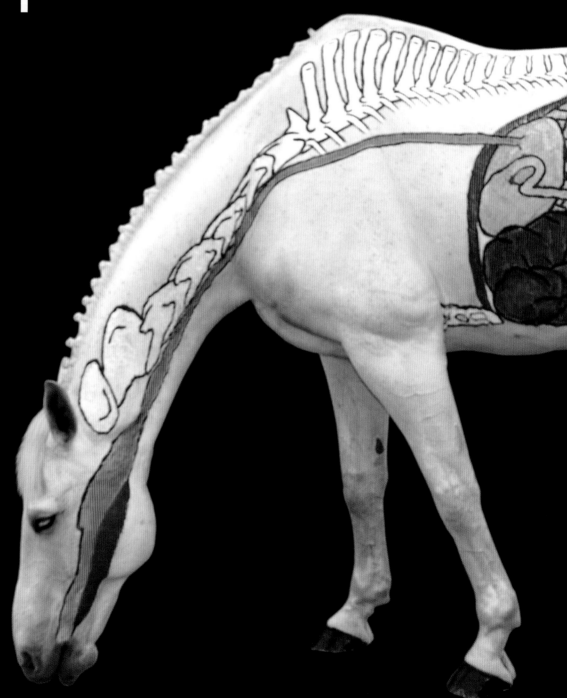

The digestive system converts food to fuel for energy and performance.

THE DIGESTIVE SYSTEM

By nature the horse is a browsing, non-ruminant herbivore adapted to survive on poor quality roughage that is high in fibre and low in starch. The modern horse, whether kept for sport or pleasure, requires a different, higher energy diet than that of its ancestors. Hay alone can not always provide all the nutrients required for energy and performance. Consequently, feeds are often concentrated, processed, cereal-based, high in sugar and fed to a timetable. Understanding the anatomy of the digestive system will enable carers to feed more effectively, reduce the risk of intestinal problems and allow the horse to perform more efficiently.

The main function of the digestive tract is to ingest and digest food, absorb the nutrients and facilitate the removal of waste by defecation. With a simple monogastric stomach and large hindgut the horse can both digest concentrates and utilise cellulose in a similar fashion to ruminants. Food is broken down and converted into energy by mechanical, chemical, enzymatic and microbial digestion. Energy provides the fuel for movement, to form new and repair damaged tissue and to provide the body with heat.

FOREGUT

Mouth

Strong, prehensile, sensitive lips sort through and grasp food which is then sheared by the incisor teeth and moved further back in the mouth to be chewed in an elliptical movement by the premolars and molars. Chewing initiates the production of saliva from the mandibular, parotid and sublingual glands which softens, moistens and lubricates the food in preparation for its journey through the digestive tract. As it contains calcium bicarbonate, saliva is slightly alkaline. This is the first defence in offsetting acidity in the stomach. Unlike humans, the horse's saliva does not contain enzymes. 10–12 litres of saliva are produced each day and this is directly proportional to the number of chews. A horse left with no food does not chew and therefore produces little saliva. Chewing is an innate psychological behaviour and horses left without food may start to chew on other things.

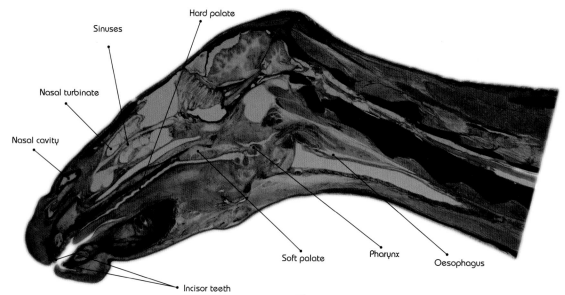

Sinuses · Hard palate · Nasal turbinate · Nasal cavity · Soft palate · Pharynx · Oesophagus · Incisor teeth

The tongue manoeuvres the food to the oropharynx at the back of the mouth where it is formed into a bolus. Together with the pharyngeal muscles it is then pushed into the oesophagus.

Teeth

The number of teeth vary but on average, an adult mare has 40 and the male 42. These grow constantly until between the ages of 25 and 30.

Deciduous or milk teeth are replaced between 2½ and 5 years. This can be painful and affect training at a time when a young horse is just starting work. Some horses also have 'wolf' teeth, found just in front of the premolars, which can cause pain if they are knocked by the bit.

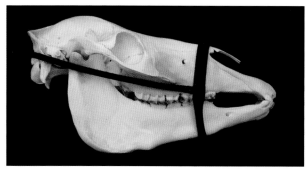

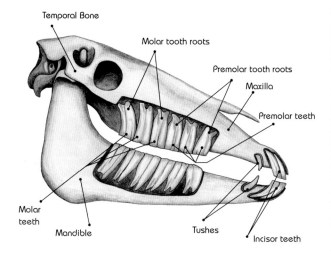

Temporal Bone
Molar tooth roots
Premolar tooth roots
Maxilla
Premolar teeth
Molar teeth
Mandible
Tushes
Incisor teeth

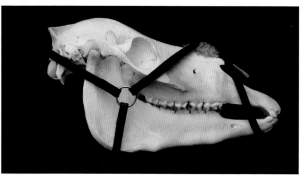

It is wise to avoid tight cavesson nosebands (*top*) with young horses as these can interfere with the molar teeth roots. A high-sided or mexican grackle (*above*) will avoid this area.

To grind feed efficiently and allow bacteria to attack the plant cell walls, teeth need to be healthy. Grass, the horse's natural food, contains silica, a hard abrasive substance which constantly wears down teeth.

Two main modern day practices result in uneven or insufficient wear on the teeth causing painful hooks, ramps, ulcers, cheek abrasions, sore gums and even jaw misalignment.

1. A softer diet and the fact that the horse eats for fewer hours means less chewing.
2. Feeding from high haynets causes the lower jaw to slide back altering the alignment of the teeth and chewing patterns.

Signs of mouth discomfort include:
• quidding, reluctance or turning the head to one side to eat
• excessive salivation or blood in saliva
• foul smell from the mouth or nose
• dull coat, weight loss, and loss of condition
• facial swelling

Performance related problems can include:
• resistance to being bridled
• head tossing or tilting
• resistance to bend or collection
• dropping behind the bit
• opening the mouth

To help prevent dental problems, it is important that teeth are checked by a veterinarian or equine dental technician every six months.

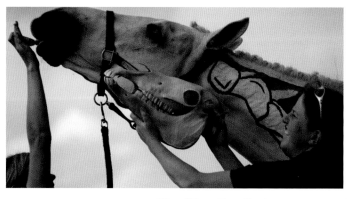

Oesophagus

This musculomembranous tube is approximately 125–150cm long. It runs slightly left and below the trachea. The bolus is propelled from the pharynx to the stomach by waves of muscular contractions in a process known as **peristalsis**. This process occurs throughout the length of the digestive tract.

If unchewed food or a foreign object blocks the oesophagus, the horse can 'choke'. Horses who bolt their food, especially if they do not have access to water, are more likely to choke than those who eat in a more leisurely fashion.

Signs of choke include the inability to swallow, excessive salivation, heavy nasal discharge or foamy saliva containing food particles, blowing out feed through the mouth or nose, coughing and extending the neck and attempting to retch. This is a condition which necessitates veterinary attention.

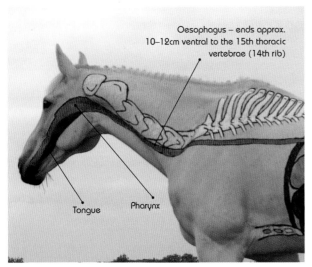

Oesophagus – ends approx. 10–12cm ventral to the 15th thoracic vertebrae (14th rib)

Tongue

Pharynx

Stomach

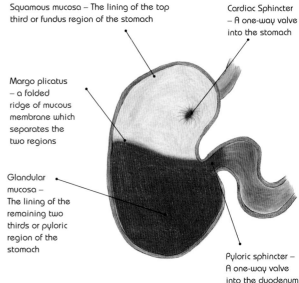

Squamous mucosa – The lining of the top third or fundus region of the stomach

Cardiac Sphincter – A one-way valve into the stomach

Margo plicatus – a folded ridge of mucous membrane which separates the two regions

Glandular mucosa – The lining of the remaining two thirds or pyloric region of the stomach

Pyloric sphincter – A one-way valve into the duodenum

Glands in the glandular mucosa secrete hydrochloric acid, pepsin and lipase which kill microbes and break down proteins and fats. They also secrete mucus which protects the pyloric region from the acidic contents of the stomach.

The stomach is relatively small. It accounts for 8–10% of the digestive system. When empty it is about the size of a rugby ball. When full, it expands as far as the 15th rib and holds 8–15 litres. It should never be more than two thirds full. Unlike humans, where the production of hydrochloric acid is stimulated by eating, horses produce a continuous flow of up to 72 litres over 24 hours even when the stomach is

Stomach Ulcers

It is estimated over 90% of stabled competition horses exhibit signs of ulcers which can reduce appetite, cause weight loss, colic, and reduced performance. The main cause is an imbalance in the aggressive elements of hydrochloric acid and pepsin and the protective factors of bicarbonate and mucous.

When grazing, or with access to ad lib hay, the stomach is rarely empty; constant chewing produces copious amounts of alkaline saliva which neutralises acid. In stabled horses left for long periods without food or fed soft concentrates, the stomach is often empty and vulnerable to attack. Concentrates also increase the hormone gastrin which stimulates and increases acid production

Another factor is starch. Horses should be fed no more than 1g per 1kg of body weight per meal. Bagged feeds often contain more than this which can lead to equine gastric ulcer syndrome and be a factor in the onset of laminitis.

The type of roughage also has an effect. Alfalfa, higher in calcium is thought to have good buffering capabilities.

Exercising on an empty stomach splashes acid onto the unprotected squamous portion. A handful of chaff prior to exercise will increase the viscosity and reduce risk.

Leisure horses with a less stressful lifestyle and greater access to turn out, have less pressure put upon their digestive system and are correspondingly less susceptible to ulcers.

empty. To mimic the natural environment where they feed for 16–20 hours per day and to offset the effects of acidity, the horse needs to be fed little and often.

As the horse is a trickle feeder, the stomach works best when it has a constant flow of digesta passing through it. Food remains in the stomach for about two hours before it passes into the small intestine. In horses fed one or two large feeds per day, the stomach will be unable to cope with the quantities and undigested food may pass into the small intestine in as little as 20 minutes. This means the best nutritional value is not being obtained from the feed. Partially digested food making its way through the digestive system also poses a greater risk of impaction.

Small Intestine

This is the major site for the enzymatic digestion where nutrients from the digested food are further degraded and absorbed into the bloodstream. It is approximately 21 metres in length, has a capacity of 40–50 litres and accounts for about 30% of the weight of the digestive tract. The alkaline requirements, which allow the digestive enzymes in the small intestine to function correctly, are produced by pancreatic juice from the pancreas and bile from the liver. Most of the fats, protein, about 50–70% of soluble carbohydrates, as well as vitamins and minerals, are absorbed here. Chyme (partially digested food) passes through the small intestine in about 90 minutes although it can take as little as 45 minutes or as long as 3 hours. The longer the chyme stays in the small intestine, the more nutrients are absorbed and the more value is obtained from the food.

There are three parts to the small intestine:
1. **The Duodenum,** which is about one metre in length. Bile, pancreatic juices and enzymes from the intestinal wall break starch and other soluble carbohydrates to glucose, proteins to amino acids and fats to fatty acids and glycerol.

2. **The Jejunum**, at about 19 metres long, is the longest section, and the chemical breakdown of chyme is completed here. Glucose, amino acids, fatty acids, glycerol, vitamins and minerals are all absorbed into the bloodstream from the jejunum to be used by the cells or stored in the liver.
3. **The Ileum**, the last metre of the small intestine, continues the process of digestion. Its main function is to absorb nutrients and control the flow of partially digested food into the caecum. Muscular contractions and peristalsis then continue to push the food on its journey.

Cross-section of a villi from the small intestines

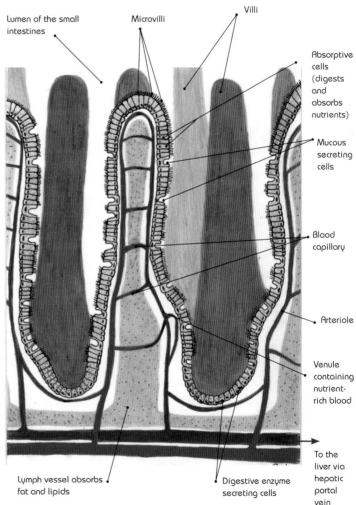

Lumen of the small intestines

Microvilli

Villi

Absorptive cells (digests and absorbs nutrients)

Mucous secreting cells

Blood capillary

Arteriole

Venule containing nutrient-rich blood

To the liver via hepatic portal vein

Lymph vessel absorbs fat and lipids

Digestive enzyme secreting cells

The lining of the small intestine is covered with villi, thin hair like structures which aid absorption of nutrients by increasing the surface area. Glands between the villi secrete large quantities of enzymes, which contribute to the breakdown of chyme.

THE LIVER

Three main ways the liver aids digestion are:

1. Producing and secreting bile
About 10 litres of bile, which flows continuously into the duodenum via the bile duct, is produced per day. Bile contains protein, cholesterol and salts. Its main function is to emulsify fats, breaking them down into smaller particles for enzymatic digestion. As a browsing herbivore with no requirement for bile to be stored, the horse has no gall bladder.

2. Metabolising nutrients
Nutrients from the intestines are transported to the liver in the blood via the hepatic portal vein. The liver absorbs and regulates the levels of protein, carbohydrate and fat by either releasing the nutrients, which are controlled by insulin and hormones, back into the blood stream as required or, by storing the excess.

    The liver also stores vitamins, minerals and glycogen which is converted to glucose for energy when required.

3. Detoxyfying and removing harmful and waste products
Any toxins, bacteria or poisons absorbed in the intestines are delivered to the liver via the hepatic portal vein. Toxins come from a variety of sources, such as mouldy, contaminated hay or feed or worm infestations. Overuse of drugs such as 'bute, steroids or even wormers can have a detrimental effect on the liver. Products such as lactic acid and ammonia are rendered harmless, converted to urea and then excreted via the kidneys in the urine.

    Although not directly related to digestion, another vital function of the liver is to regulate blood proteins which gives the blood viscosity and allows it to clot.

Worms

Different parasites are found throughout the digestive tract. Controlling them is essential for the health and efficient functioning of the entire system. In large numbers worms can contribute to loss of condition, weight loss, anaemia, diarrhoea, coughing, colic and declining performance. Worms can be controlled by a combination of pasture management and regular worming, although no drug kills every type of worm and some strains are becoming increasingly drug resistant. For accuracy of diagnosis a regular faecal worm egg count ensures a direct, targeted and effective de-worming programme.

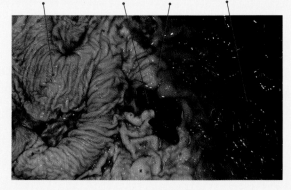

Squamous mucosa   Bot larvae   Margo Plicatus   Glandular mucosa

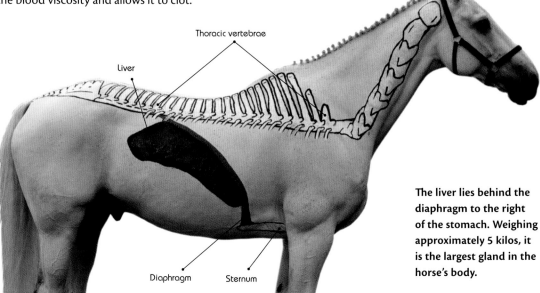

Thoracic vertebrae

Liver

Diaphragm   Sternum

The liver lies behind the diaphragm to the right of the stomach. Weighing approximately 5 kilos, it is the largest gland in the horse's body.

Liver Damage

Horses are not designed to be overburdened by excessive amounts of nutrients, proteins, vitamins or drugs, all of which can lead to liver malfunction and disease. Fortunately the liver has a remarkable capacity to regenerate. Hepatocytes, specialised large cells, perform most of the liver's work. These cells die and are replaced by new cells on a regular basis.

Ragwort poisoning is the most common cause of equine liver damage in the UK. Other causes are bacteria, chemical toxins and tumours. Ragwort, a biennial plant, produces thousands of wind borne seeds that allow the plant to spread rapidly. The toxic compound pyrrolizidine found in the plant damages liver cells which can no longer produce the proteins necessary to regenerate. These are then replaced by non-functional fibrous tissue. The effect is cumulative causing irreversible malfunction as the liver shrinks. The liver cannot function at less than 30% and once this size is reached, signs of liver disease, which can be verified by a blood test, appear rapidly and the outcome is inevitable.

Signs of liver failure, whatever the cause, include poor performance, loss of appetite, depression, diarrhoea, weight loss, sensitivity to sunlight, jaundice, swelling under the abdomen, weakness and neurological indicators including yawning, head pressing, confusion, unco-ordinated movement, ataxia and fitting. Once the symptoms appear the illness can last from a week to several months.

Most horses will avoid ragwort, although some do acquire a taste for the bitterness of the plant. Seedlings develop in the autumn, rosettes appear in spring and the mature plant flowers from May to October. Buttercups and hay containing ragwort also pose a threat.

THE PANCREAS

The pancreatic duct continuously secretes pancreatic juice into the duodenum and hormones into the bloodstream. The most important hormones are insulin and glucagon which regulate blood sugar levels. When blood glucose rises, insulin, released from the beta cells, causes glucose to enter body cells to be used for energy. Pancreatic juice contains sodium bicarbonate which reduces the acidity of the gut.

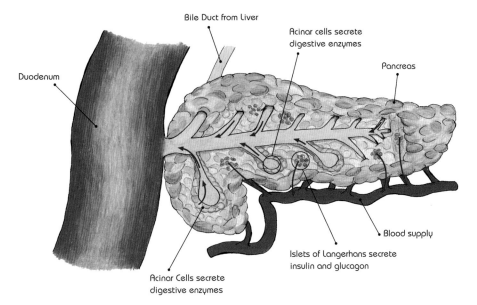

Bile Duct from Liver
Acinar cells secrete digestive enzymes
Pancreas
Duodenum
Blood supply
Islets of Langerhans secrete insulin and glucagon
Acinar Cells secrete digestive enzymes

The Digestive System

THE HINDGUT

The hindgut needs to be large to digest the large quantities of cellulose found in forage. It is extremely heavy, weighing around a third of the horse's total bodyweight. It is the weight of the gut that is responsible for the evolution of a rigid spine to support it; a fact which also allows the horse to carry the weight of the rider.

The hindgut serves as a reservoir of water and electrolytes, vital to sustain exercise performance.

A by-product of cellulose breakdown in the hindgut is heat. In cold weather it is important to make sure horses have access to plenty of fibre to help keep them warm.

The Large Intestines

The large intestine is approximately 8 metres long. Made up of the caecum, large and small colon and rectum, it accounts for 60% of the digestive tract. Similar to that of a ruminant, and with a large population of friendly bacteria, this fermentation chamber digests plant fibre and insoluble carbohydrates. It also absorbs vitamins, minerals, water and electrolytes essential for exercise and performance. It is sacculated in appearance.

Caecum

Undigested, insoluble carbohydrates enter the caecum through the ileo-caecal valve. This large sac, which lies on the right dorsal side of abdomen, makes up approximately 25% of the large intestine and has a capacity of up to 35 litres. Millions of micro-organisms, (bacteria, yeasts, fungi and protozoa) break down the indigestible cellulose and fibrous remains of food into a form that can be absorbed by the caecum. The bacterial population specialises in digesting a particular type of food and varies according to diet, for example, horses fed forage have different bacteria to those fed concentrates. A change in diet needs to be introduced slowly to allow the bacteria sufficient time to adjust and to avoid stomach upsets.

After fermentation in the caecum, food enters the colon.

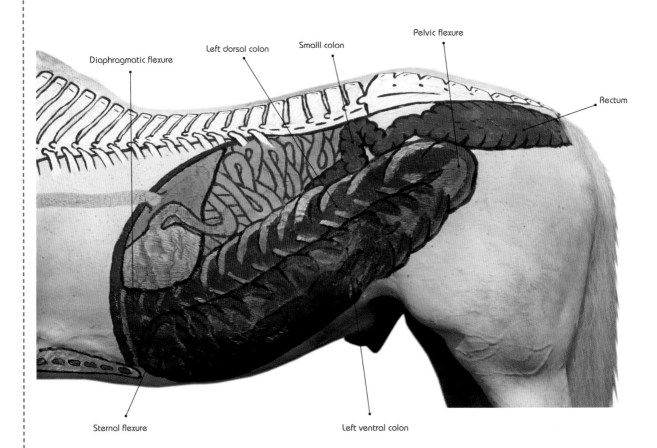

Diaphragmatic flexure

Left dorsal colon

Smalll colon

Pelvic flexure

Rectum

Sternal flexure

Left ventral colon

Large Colon

The large colon is 3.5 metres long with a capacity of about 90 litres. Microbial digestion continues breaking down the tough fibrous forage and cellulose. The large colon is also the main site for the absorption of nutrients and water. Twists and turns, together with the variable diameter, make the passage of food through the colon slow. There are four parts with three sharp U-bends within the large colon. These are known as the **sternal**, **pelvic** and **diaphragmatic flexures** and are prime sites for impaction colic. The pelvic flexure, which has the greatest reduction in diameter in addition to its 180 degree bend, is a particularly common site as partially digested food, often as a result of an overload of concentrates or unchewed food from horses with dental problems, makes its way through the system. Fewer problems occur when the horse is fed grass or hay.

Colic, or intestinal pain, can also result from the formation of gas derived from inappropriate microbial fermentation.

Maintaining the Microbial Population

Stress, travelling, competitions, a change of diet, the use of wormers, medicines and antibiotics all alter the environment of the hindgut killing off many of the micro organisms. This can reduce digestive efficiency and cause upsets which are reflected in performance. To avoid this consider a pro and prebiotic supplement. Probiotics stimulate the growth of 'friendly bacteria' which benefit the intestinal flora. Prebiotics are non-digestible and promote the growth of beneficial micro organisms in the intestines.

Small Colon

With a capacity of 20 litres, the small colon, a continuation of the large colon, is 3.5 metres long and has a reduced diameter. Moving freely and intertwined with the jejunum, it is susceptible to twisting. Its main function is to absorb water, electrolytes and nutrients and to prepare matter for excretion.

Rectum

Food residue finally passes into the rectum which is a storage place for faeces before it exits the system. Beginning at the pelvic inlet and terminating at the anus, the rectum is approximately 30cm in length and is usually straight.

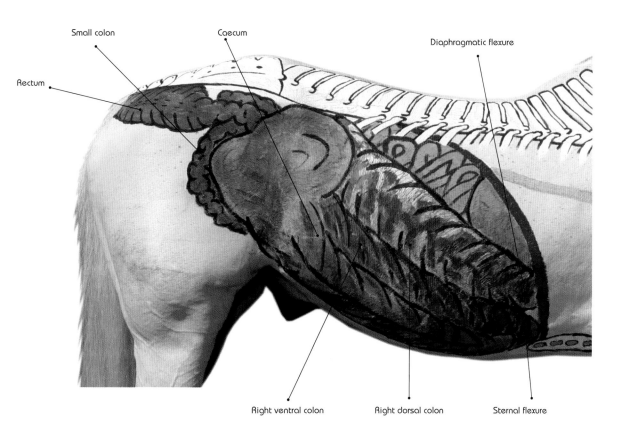

Small colon · Caecum · Diaphragmatic flexure · Rectum · Right ventral colon · Right dorsal colon · Sternal flexure

The Digestive System

DIET, DIGESTION, EXERCISE AND PERFORMANCE

Water

Access to fresh, clean **water** is crucial. Approximately 70% of the body is water. This is lost through urine, faeces, breathing and sweat. When lost in large quantities through heat or work it needs to be replaced with electrolytes (see page 13).

Energy

Energy is required for speed, stamina, condition, muscular strength and endurance. The success of the performance horse relies heavily on the supply of energy and its utilisation.

For optimal digestive function, horses require a balanced diet which will ensure a healthy weight, and enough energy for growth, work and repair. As a rule of thumb, typical daily intake needs to be between 1.5 and 2.5% of the total body mass. This means a 700kg horse should consume between 10.5 and 17.5kg of hay per day. Food should be fed by weight not volume. To mimic the natural environment, the horse should have access to forage for at least 16 hours per day. Bucket feeds should ideally be given little and often to prevent overload, wastage and the risk of intestinal upsets. Horses that are overfed can become overweight, have reduced energy and additional pressure may be placed on the heart, lungs and legs.

Energy is derived from two main sources:

1. Carbohydrate is the main fuel for optimum performance. There are three forms:

1. **Cellulose**, which can only be digested by the millions of microbes found in the hindgut, is the fibre found in tough, long-stemmed grasses and roughage. It is essential for the correct functioning of the digestive system and produces steady, slow release energy. No horse can do without it.
2. **Starch**, found in grains and legumes, is easier to digest as it is broken down and absorbed in the small intestine to produce quick release energy. Traditionally, greater energy demands have been met by starch in the form of cereal grains. As an excess of starch can be damaging to the horse, it is now thought this can be provided more safely in the form of highly digestible fibre such as sugar beet or oil.
3. **Sugar** is found in cereal such as oats and corn, lush grasses, particularly in spring and early summer, molasses, carrots and apples. As soluble carbohydrate, sugars are most easily digested in the stomach and small intestine. They provide a source of immediate energy.

Feeding requirements for leisure horses are relatively simple. They require roughage in the form of grass or hay. Requirements for sports horses can be more complex. It is essential that a balanced ration is formulated taking account of weight, condition, workload, environmental temperature and age. A horse that works consistently or finds it difficult to maintain weight will need both forage and concentrate food to sustain energy. The harder and faster a horse works the more energy he requires.

2. Oils and Fats provide energy rich feed for working, performance, lactating or growing horses. They also add body condition as they have around three times as many calories as carbohydrate. Oils and fats are an excellent type of 'fuel' for endurance horses or those horses that become over excitable on grain, as they are a slow-release energy source. A horse in heavy work may benefit from fat or oil supplementation.

Exercise and the Digestive System

Exercise has a positive effect on the digestive system by increasing metabolism. It also has a beneficial effect on the body's ability to utilise insulin and therefore exercise. Even simple, short bouts of walking are essential for horses and ponies suffering from laminitis, Cushing's syndrome, equine metabolic syndrome and insulin resistance. During exercise the sympathetic nervous system diverts blood from the digestive system to the muscles (see page 116).

Inadequate energy in the diet can have a negative effect on performance.

Protein

Protein is important for growth and repair. It forms the building blocks of bones, muscles, cartilage and skin. It is also essential for the structure of red blood cells, for the proper functioning of antibodies, resisting infection and for the regulation of enzymes and hormones. It is particularly important for foals, pregnant and lactating mares. Forages contain 8–20% protein and are sufficient for maintenance. Additional protein in the form of soya, beans, peas and linseed are found in bagged feeds. In horses subjected to starvation, once all the fat stores are used up, the muscles are broken down and the protein is used for energy.

Vitamins and Minerals

A vitamin is an organic compound that is needed in small quantities to manage the chemical reactions that occur in the body. Naturally occurring vitamins and minerals form an important part of a horse's diet and seldom need to be supplemented. They do not generate energy.

Feeding is a science and an art. Correct balance and feeding management is important to ensure that the nutritional needs of the horse are met. There is a plethora of ready mixed, balanced feeds available on the market, the content of which is advertised on the bag. Before embarking on a feeding programme, advice should be sought from an independent nutritionist.

Practical Application

- Ensure the horse has as much turn out as possible.
- Provide a clean, constant supply of water.
- Feed hay in different corners of the stable to keep the horse moving.
- Feed from the floor. This ensures correct alignment of the jaw, aids digestion, ensures correct positioning of the back, drains the sinuses correctly, slows the intake of food and ensures correct functioning of the respiratory system.
- For a healthy digestive system, at least 75% of the diet should be forage.
- It is important to balance the anatomical requirement for forage with the energy requirement of concentrate.
- Too little forage and too much concentrate in stabled horses leads to boredom, stress, reduced bowel efficiency, intestinal overload, weight gain and digestive imbalance.
- Feed something succulent when grass is poor.
- Never feed mouldy or contaminated feeds. This can cause digestive upsets, coughs, respiratory illnesses and colic.
- Ensure hay does not contain poisonous weeds.

Soaking hay for one hour removes dust and spores which can cause coughs and respiratory problems. Soaked for more than two hours, up to 70% of the nutritional value is lost. This is useful for removing sugar for overweight horses but wasteful for horses requiring the full nutritional value. In this case a better option may be a hay steamer.

SUMMARY

- Horses have a unique digestive tract that can digest both forage and concentrates.
- Long-stemmed forages such as hay are necessary in the diet to ensure normal digestive function.
- The small intestine is the site of enzymatic digestion of soluble carbohydrates, proteins and fats, the components of which are absorbed into the circulation.
- Insoluble carbohydrates pass into the caecum and colon where they are fermented by micro organisms similar to those in the fore stomach of the ruminant.

- Correct feeding management is important to ensure that the nutritional needs are met.
- Give a handful of chaff before exercise to reduce the risk of stomach ulcers.
- To avoid dietary upsets or metabolic disorders, and to allow bacteria in the hindgut time to adapt, changes in feed should be introduced gradually.
- As a trickle feeder, the challenge for horse owners is to balance nature with the fact that many horses are now stabled and are subjected to the routine that this involves.

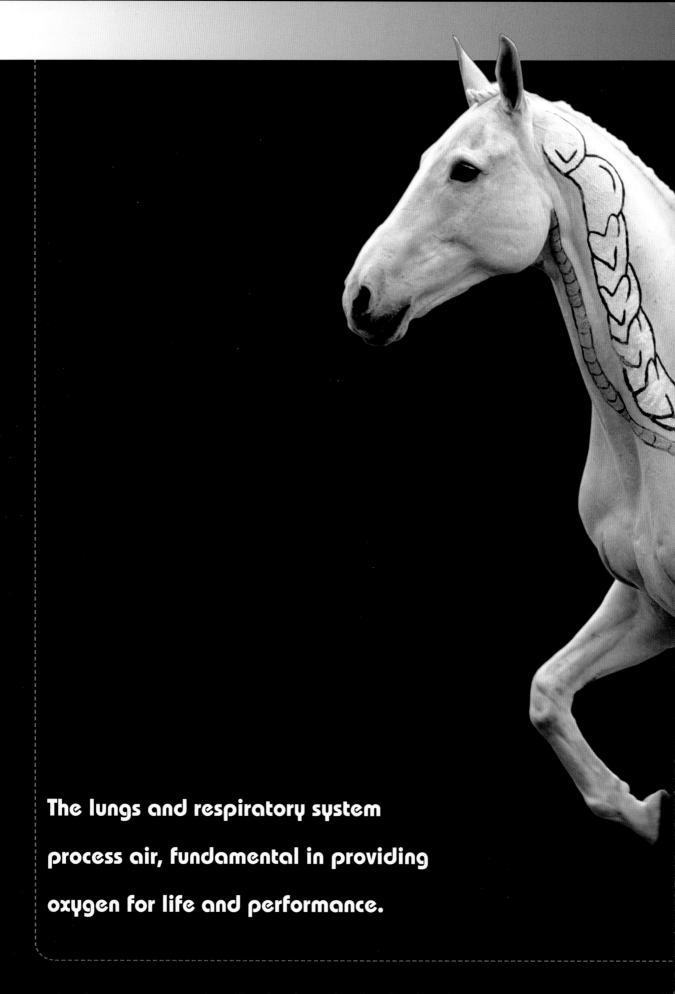

The lungs and respiratory system
process air, fundamental in providing
oxygen for life and performance.

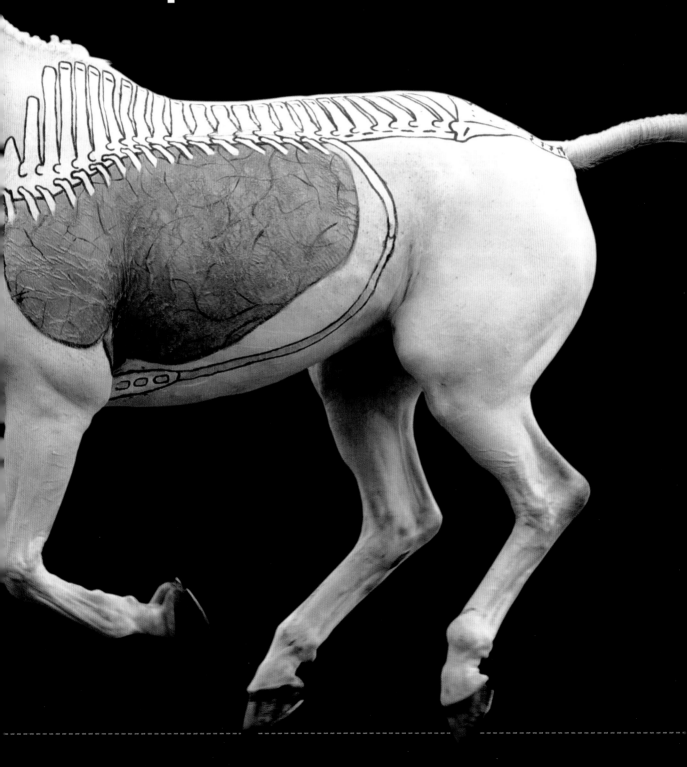

The Respiratory System

THE RESPIRATORY SYSTEM

Respiration is the act of inhaling and exhaling air. Oxygen is vital for life and cells need a continual supply to enable them to release energy from food. For an equine athlete to provide sustained performance, blood must assimilate oxygen from the lungs and transport it efficiently to the muscles. This is an important consideration in how we manage, condition and train our horses. Basically, the more efficient this process is, the more stamina the horse will have and the more mentally alert he will be.

The respiratory system consists of:
• the upper respiratory tract – the nostrils, nasal passages, sinuses and larynx
• the lower respiratory tract – the windpipe (trachea), lungs, bronchi, bronchioles, and diaphragm

The main function of the respiratory system is to:
• bring oxygen into the lungs and transfer it to the blood stream where it is distributed around the body via the circulatory system (see page 88)
• exchange oxygen for carbon dioxide, a toxic waste product from the cells which must be quickly and efficiently removed
• regulate breathing to control internal carbon dioxide levels
• regulate hydration by removing excess water from the body as the horse breathes out
• assist thermoregulation by breathing hot air out and bringing cool air in
• facilitate the sense of smell
• allow communication by neighing, snorting and squealing.

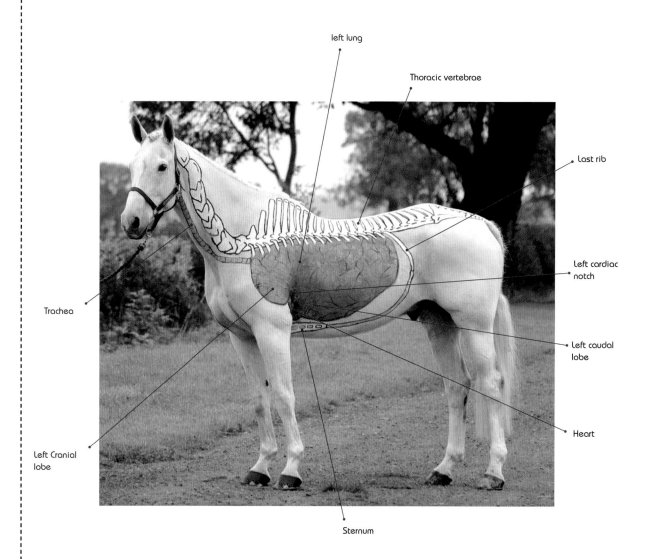

left lung

Thoracic vertebrae

Last rib

Left cardiac notch

Left caudal lobe

Heart

Trachea

Left Cranial lobe

Sternum

THE UPPER RESPIRATORY TRACT

Nostrils and Nasal Passages

Air is drawn into the nasal cavities through the nostrils as the horse cannot breathe through his mouth. These cavities are separated from the mouth by the hard palate which is made of bone and forms the roof of the mouth and base of the nasal cavity. Air is filtered and cleaned in the nasal cavities by a moist mucous membrane and tiny hairs called cilia. These move in a Mexican-wave type action, pushing dust, germs and debris back up into the throat (pharynx) where it drains out of the nostrils and is swallowed or coughed up.

Normal nasal discharge is translucent and relatively thin. More will be seen during or after heavier exercise.

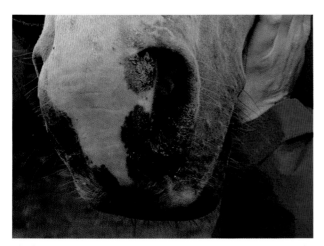

Thick, coloured or increased mucous discharge is not normal and should be investigated.

The Sense of Smell

The horse has a very strong sense of smell. The nostrils have the capacity to expand or 'flare' to draw in more air as exertion increases. This also allows the horse to draw in more scents. The olfactory receptors, consisting of a group of millions of specialised, elongated nerve cells known as the vomeronasal organ, located in the mucous membrane of the upper nasal cavity chemically analyse the smell. The horse makes sense of much of his environment through smell which he uses to recognise friends and foe. He can even 'smell' danger in the form of pheromones secreted by stressed or fearful companions or riders!

When a horse raises his head and curls his lip, he is closing the nostrils to trap and memorise strong or unfamiliar scents. This is known as the 'flehman' posture. It is often observed in stallions during the breeding season to assess the breeding status of a mare (see page 143).

The horse has a long memory and can remember the scent of people and substances. Once he has memorised the smell of something in his feed, for example, it is almost impossible to persuade him to eat it no matter how cleverly it is disguised. This is an important consideration when encouraging a horse to take medication in feed.

The Respiratory System

The Pharynx

The pharynx is a chamber lined with mucous membrane at the throat which connects the nasal passages to the larynx. The soft palate, a muscular continuation of the hard palate, separates the oesophagus, which takes food to the stomach, and the larynx, which takes air to the trachea.

The Larynx

The larynx, suspended from the base of the skull by the hyoid apparatus, connects the pharynx to the trachea. It controls the airflow into the lungs during breathing and is protected by five rings of cartilage that can be felt between the two lower jawbones. The rings provide areas for muscle attachments which open and close the epiglottis, rather like a lid, allowing the horse to swallow and preventing foreign bodies from entering the trachea. The tongue, which pushes food to the back of the mouth, stimulates epiglottis closure and swallowing. If the horse gets his tongue 'over the bit', it can restrict his breathing and even close the larynx. The tongue is also attached to the hyoid apparatus and some neck flexor muscles that run down the base of the neck. Any tension, restriction, or peculiar movement of the tongue therefore, can affect the way of going.

The larynx also houses the vocal chords which, when vibrated by the forced passage of air, allows the horse to whinny, nicker and neigh. Any paralysis in the muscles that control the vocal cords can restrict airflow resulting in whistling or roaring. The left side is more prone to damage than the right, as the nerve serving the muscle takes a longer route and is therefore more susceptible to damage.

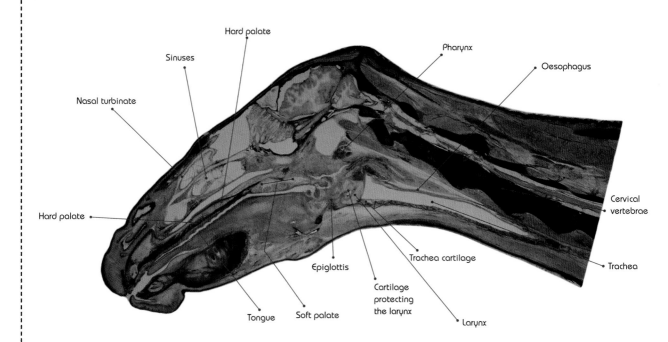

Within the nasal passages, turbine bones, which are thin, convoluted pieces of cartilage, increase turbulence warming and cleaning the air before passing it through the pharynx, larynx and trachea.

THE LOWER RESPIRATORY TRACT

Trachea and Bronchi

The trachea is a continuation of the larynx. In the adult horse it can be up to 1 metre long, extending as far as the 4th thoracic vertebrae. It is 5cm in diameter and held open by 50–60 horseshoe-shaped, cartilaginous rings, which are embedded into the wall. These rings form a continuous tube which can be felt along the underside of the neck. The trachea is separated from the vertebrae by the oesophagus which lies on the open side of the trachea cartilages and expands with the passage of food. The trachea divides into two bronchi just above the heart.

The Lungs –The Main Organ of Respiration

Each bronchi passes into a lung, the left being slightly smaller than the right to allow space for the heart. The lungs together with the heart and spleen fill the thorax. They are made up of an enormous surface area of convoluted, spongy, elastic tissue that increases and decreases as the horse breathes. A smooth slippery membrane, called the pleura, lines the walls of the chest cavity and the outer surface of the lungs. The space in between is filled with a lubricant, the pleural fluid, which allows the lungs to expand and contract without damage. Within the lung, the bronchi continue to divide and subdivide rather like the branches of a tree. The smallest branches of the bronchioles, scarcely larger than a hair, terminate in millions of tiny air sacs called alveoli.

Deoxygenated blood from around the body flows via the right side of the heart and pulmonary artery into the lungs through the capillaries embedded in the semi-permeable walls of the alveoli. The carbon dioxide is then extracted and exhaled as waste. Inhalation brings in fresh, dry air high in oxygen. This reaches the alveoli where it is

Facts and figures

- At rest the breathing rate of the horse is 10–18 breaths per minute (bpm). This can rise to 240bpm during maximal exercise. As well as exercise, breathing can be elevated by a rise in body temperature, pain, adrenalin and the fight flight response.
- A healthy adult horse at rest will have a respiration rate of approximately half his pulse rate. A horse with a pulse rate of 32 therefore, should have an approximate respiration rate of 16bpm.
- There are 300 million alveoli in the human lungs. These cover a surface area of 160m², which is approximately the size of a tennis court and 80 times greater than the surface area of our skin!
- The number of alveoli in a horse is estimated to be 250% greater at 750 million and would cover a football field!
- With an unrestricted upper airway and huge lung capacity air intake, a galloping horse will breathe in up to 1,800 litres of air per minute.
- At gallop, 300 litres of blood is pumped at high pressure through small lung capillaries surrounding 10 million air sacs to take up and deliver more than 70 litres of oxygen per minute to the working muscles.

absorbed by the haemoglobin in red blood cells, taken to the heart by the pulmonary vein and then pumped to the rest of the body where it is absorbed and used to unlock energy from food for use by the muscles and every other cell in the body.

This is a complex process known as gaseous exchange.

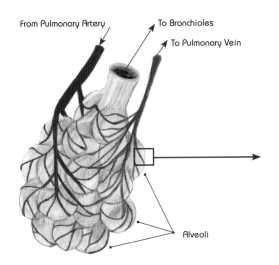

From Pulmonary Artery

To Bronchioles

To Pulmonary Vein

Alveoli

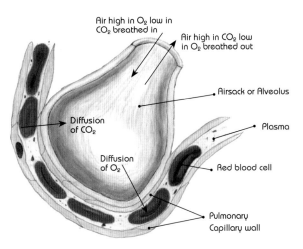

Air high in O₂ low in CO₂ breathed in

Air high in CO₂ low in O₂ breathed out

Airsack or Alveolus

Diffusion of CO₂

Plasma

Diffusion of O₂

Red blood cell

Pulmonary Capillary wall

The Respiratory System

THE MECHANICS OF BREATHING

The ribcage provides protection for the heart and lungs. During inhalation, the intercostal muscles expand the spaces between the ribs causing them to move up and out.

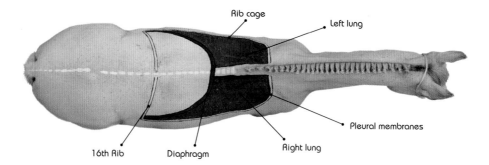

The diaphragm, a large forward facing, bowl-shaped sheet of muscle separating the chest and abdomen, contracts and flattens to enlarge the chest cavity – in some cases back as far as the 16th rib. This causes the air pressure within the lungs to fall below that of the external environment drawing air into the lungs. As the ribs return to their original position, the diaphragm relaxes to its dome shape and the volume of the chest decreases forcing air back out of the lungs. This is a similar action to a pair of bellows. The rib movement can be seen as the respiration rate increases and is particularly noticeable on thinner horses.

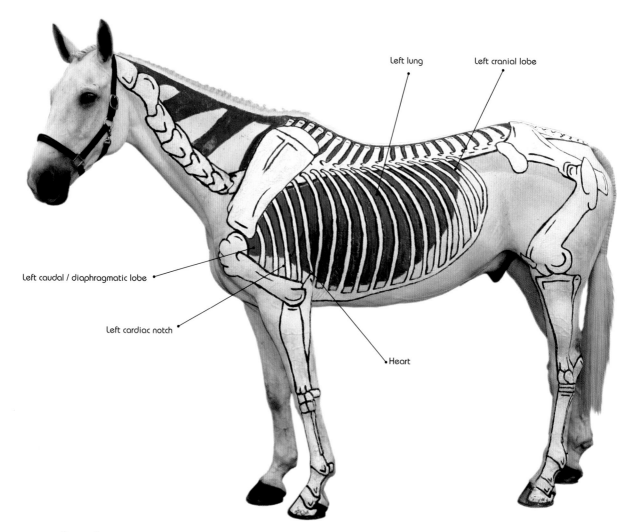

THE ROLE OF THE RESPIRATORY SYSTEM DURING EXERCISE

The mechanics of breathing in a horse being exercised is quite different to that of the resting horse. Conditioning of the respiratory and cardiovascular systems are closely linked. They work in harmony to supply the heart and working muscles increased demand for oxygen by:

- increasing the volume of inspired air – breathing in more air
- increasing cardiac output – the heart pumping harder and faster
- increased alveoli/capillary function – increased gaseous exchange
- increased dissipation of heat – hot air breathed out faster

The Effect of Neck Position on Breathing

Positioning of the head and neck influences the ability to take in air. This is something that needs to be considered particularly when training horses with upper respiratory tract dysfunction. For maximum efficiency, the airways need to be open and unrestricted. This can be seen in the galloping horse where the airway is streamlined for optimum airflow.

Partial flexion of the head and neck, required in varying degrees by show jumpers or dressage horses to improve balance and impulsion, interferes with the streamlining. A bend at the throat causes resistance to airflow as the pharynx is compressed and the trachea flexes and shortens. A horse that is 'on the bit' always loses some airway freedom.

When a horse is asked to over bend, he may struggle to optimise air intake and in order to open the airway, he may resist the rider's demands by dropping his head down to try to relieve the constriction in his pharynx. This may also cause the vocal cords to vibrate excessively in the pharynx and 'make a noise'. If the head is held in this position during faster or more demanding work, performance may well suffer. We could not run a marathon with our chin on our chest!

The diameter of the pharynx is reduced when the neck is high and the head is in a flexed position.

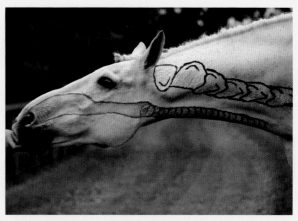

The pharyngeal diameter is optimised when the neck is extended in the midway position.

The Effect of Gait on Breathing

At walk and trot there is little relationship between respiration rate and stride.

Inhalation

When the pelvis is tilted and the hind legs brought well under the body, ready to thrust the head and forelimbs are raised, the intestines shift rearwards, the scapula moves forwards and the ribs expand as air is drawn into the lungs.

Exhalation

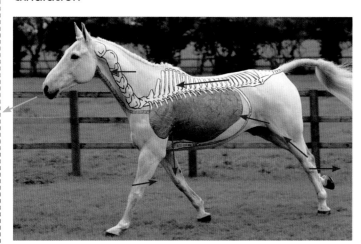

In this forward position when head is stretched out, the hindlimbs are raised, and weight is taken on the forelimbs, the contents of the abdomen are shifted forwards, pressing on the diaphragm and pushing air out. This is further aided by the fact that the scapula is pshed back further reducing the capacity of the lungs.

How the horse breathes in relation to canter and gallop

At canter and gallop respiration is synchronised with stride frequency. The maximum number of strides a horse can take is in the region of 130 per minute. As speed increases, the body's requirement for oxygen rises proportionally therefore at gallop, the respiration rate can also rise to 130 bpm. This is known as respiratory locomotive coupling. There is one breath per stride at the canter/gallop caused by the content of the gut moving forwards and backwards. Simply, the horse expels air as the fore limbs strike the ground and breathes in as he pushes with the hindlimbs.

Respiratory Fitness

Efficient lung function is essential for optimum performance. As activity intensifies through a structured fittening programme, the horse breathes faster. Factors that may limit respiratory efficiency include the volume of the lungs, the diameter of the airway and gait.

Factors Influencing Respiratory Fitness

- With exercise, the amount of air breathed in and out with each breath, the tidal volume, increases the amount of oxygen brought into the lungs to be extracted by gaseous exchange and delivered to the heart and vascular system.
- As fitness increases, a greater percentage of the alveoli open up. This is known as alveolar recruitment and increases the capacity for gaseous exchange.
- The more efficiently oxygen is delivered to the bloodstream for use by cells and exercising muscles, the more stamina and mental willingness the horse will display.
- Aerobic exercise improves respiratory and circulatory function by increasing oxygen consumption.
- Improved capillary development across the alveoli will facilitate more efficient gaseous exchange.

- The pH of the blood. The more carbon dioxide there is in the blood, the harder the horse has to breathe to get rid of the excess.
- As a horse becomes fitter, the muscles of the heart will strengthen and supply more oxygen to the cells and skeletal muscles.
- As muscles become fitter, they do not need to work as hard to produce effort.
- The efficiency of the diaphragm improves.

Heat Dissipation through Respiration

A raised respiratory rate encourages the horse to 'blow' off heat accumulated through exercise. This is exacerbated in warm humid conditions. Fast, shallow breaths up to 140bpm facilitate heat loss by convection, conduction and evaporation, by increasing the airflow within the nostrils.

Respiratory Recovery Rate

Following strenuous exercise it is advisable to keep the horse walking until his respiration rate returns to normal. This varies from horse to horse although following strenuous exercise both the respiratory and heart rates should have recovered after 20–30 minutes. To establish individual baseline parameters, keep a log of the heart and respiration rate before and after each training session. As fittening work progresses, the rates should return to normal with shorter cool down times. If the rates deviate from the norm, it may be necessary to investigate. As a raised respiration rate causes the skeletal muscles to work harder thus creating more heat, it is important to cool the body down as quickly as possible. Cool water warms quickly once it is in contact with the skin so it is important to apply, then remove and reapply, until the temperature comes down and respiration returns to normal.

MANAGEMENT FOR A HEALTHY RESPIRATORY SYSTEM

Respiratory dysfunction is second only to musculoskeletal injuries as a cause of poor performance in athletic horses. Problems relating to the lower respiratory system are generally the result of viral, bacterial or allergic reactions. To minimise risk:

- **Use only high-quality, uncontaminated, dust and mould-free hay and bedding**. Allergens can damage sections of the bronchioles and alveoli, which can dramatically reduce the area of the lungs available for transfer of oxygen to the blood. Using a hay steamer is extremely effective at minimising dust, bacteria, mould and yeast content of hay.
- **Feed from the floor** to allow mucous to drain from the nostrils. Keep the airways open to allow the respiratory tract to function as nature intended.
- **Keep the stable clean and well ventilated**. Decomposing urine and faeces increase ammonia levels that are linked to poor respiratory health.
- **Only clean the stable and replenish the bed when the horse is outside**. This avoids inhalation of dust, pollens and other allergens.
- **Turn the horse out as much as possible.**
- **Worm regularly**. Intestinal parasites can lead to anaemia, which can be detected by having a regular blood count. A decrease in red blood cells will result in a reduced uptake of oxygen for use by the body causing the horse to become lethargic and unresponsive.

- **Assess conformation prior to purchase**. Look for large nostrils, a wide space between the front legs and the width of the ribcage, as these are all good indicators of lung capacity.

SUMMARY

- Efficient respiratory function is essential for optimum performance.
- Gaseous exchange takes place in the lungs.
- The lungs assist in temperature control.
- Respiratory system dysfunction is an important cause of exercise intolerance and poor performance.
- Damage to the lungs cannot be rectified by training.
- Breathing is linked to gait in canter and gallop.
- Head and neck position affects respiratory function.

A strong healthy heart is

essential for performance.

The Cardiovascular System

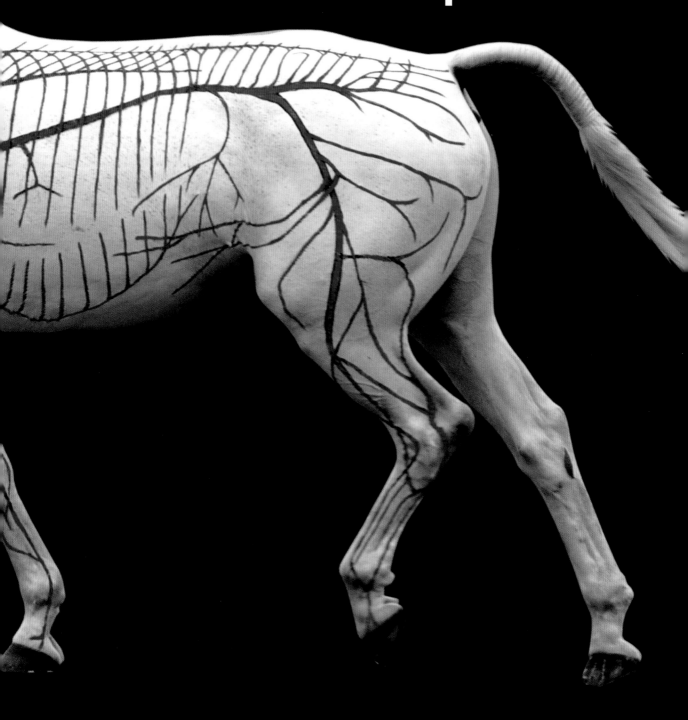

BLOOD

Approximately 45 litres of blood, which accounts for 10% of body mass, circulates around the body. The main component is **plasma**, a straw coloured liquid which suspends:

- **Red Blood Cells** or **Erythrocytes** which contain the pigment haemoglobin, produced in bone marrow. They transport oxygen and carbon dioxide to and from the tissues.
- **White Blood Cells** or **Leukocytes.** Less numerous than erythrocytes, they originate in the red bone marrow and lymph system, accumulate at sites of infection and produce antibodies to defend the body against bacteria and disease.
- **Platelets** or **Thrombocytes**. These make up a very small amount of the blood, repair damaged blood vessels and produce a blood clotting agent.
- **Fats, carbohydrates, proteins, chemical substances** and **hormones**.

A healthy cardiovascular system enables the horse to be energetic, strong and full of joie de vivre.

Definition

Cardiovascular stems from the Greek word *kardi* which means 'heart' and the Latin word *vasculum* which means 'small vessel'. The cardiovascular system uses the heart and blood vessels to circulate the blood around the body.

The Blood's Role in Thermoregulation

The horse maintains his core temperature of 38°C through a variety of means (see page 12). Heat from the muscles or core is distributed, utilised or dissipated through capillary vasodilation and vasoconstriction as required. The volume of blood within the skin affects the temperature. Arterioles close to the skin can contract or expand to control blood flow. If the horse becomes hot, the hypothalamus (see page 125) directs the sympathetic nerves to dilate the arterioles bringing blood to the surface. Heat is then lost through conduction and radiation. If the horse becomes cold, the diameter of the arterioles narrows, lessening the amount of blood at the surface and reducing heat loss.

Vasodilation

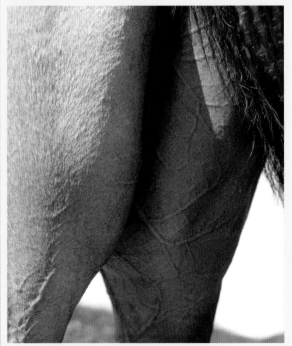

THE HEART

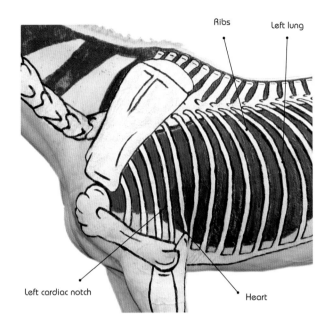

Ribs

Left lung

Left cardiac notch

Heart

The heart is made up of three layers of specialised cardiac muscle:

1. The **endocardium**, the inner lining.
2. The **myocardium**, the main muscular tissue responsible for the contraction of the heart.
3. The **pericardium**, a fluid-filled sac like membrane surrounding the heart.

The heart is divided into four chambers. The upper two, the atria, are less muscular and send blood to the lower chambers, which are more muscular. The left ventricle is the most muscular as it has to pump blood under pressure vast distances around the body. A muscular wall called the septum separates the right and left sides of the heart.

There are four valves within the heart which prevent backflow into the previous chamber. They are the:

• **Tricuspid valve** at the exit of the right atrium
• **Bicuspid valve** at the exit of the left atrium
• **Pulmonary semilunar valve** at the exit of the right ventricle
• **Aortic semilunar valve** at the exit of the left ventricle.

The heart, the first organ to form in the embryo, is the most important organ in the body. It is a hollow cone shaped muscle weighing about 4.5 kilograms and is situated between the lungs to the left of the chest within the protective walls of the ribcage. As the horse gets fitter, the size and weight may increase. A wide chest allows more space for the heart and lungs which suggests greater athletic potential.

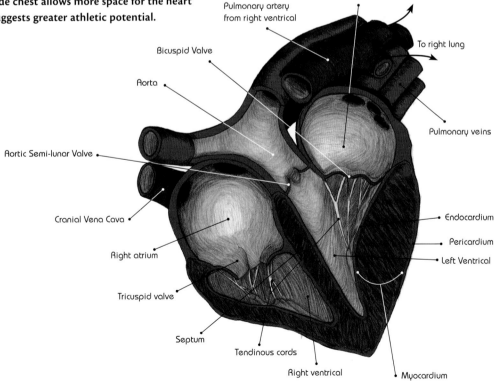

Left atrium

To left lung

Pulmonary artery from right ventrical

To right lung

Bicuspid Valve

Aorta

Pulmonary veins

Aortic Semi-lunar Valve

Endocardium

Pericardium

Cranial Vena Cava

Left Ventrical

Right atrium

Tricuspid valve

Septum

Tendinous cords

Right ventrical

Myocardium

The Cardiovascular System

The Heartbeat

The opening and closing of the valves are heard as the heart beat, making a sound similar to 'lub-dup'. The 'lub' is caused by the closing of the bicuspid and tricuspid valves and the 'dup' is caused by the snapping shut of the semilunar valves. The action of the heart muscle relaxing before and during the process of filling is known as the diastolic action. The contraction of the heart muscle as it empties is known as systolic action.

The Heart as a Pump

Oxygenated blood is brought to the left atrium via the pulmonary veins from the lungs. It is then squeezed through the bicuspid valve into the left ventricle. From there it exits the heart through the aortic semilunar valve and is pumped via the aorta to all areas of the body apart from the lungs.

Simultaneously, deoxygenated blood is brought to the right atrium via the vena cava. It is squeezed into the right ventricle through the tricuspid valve, exits the heart through the pulmonary semilunar valve and is pumped via the pulmonary artery to the lungs for gaseous exchange.

Once emptied, the heart relaxes and refills. The entire process takes only a fraction of a second and is controlled by involuntary electrical impulses created by a pacemaker located on the right of the right atrium.

Two systems pump the blood simultaneously around the body:

1. **The Pulmonary Circulation** takes deoxygenated blood from the heart to the lungs and brings oxygenated blood back to the heart.
2. **The Systemic Circulation** takes the oxygen rich blood from the heart to the rest of the body and brings deoxygenated blood back to the heart.

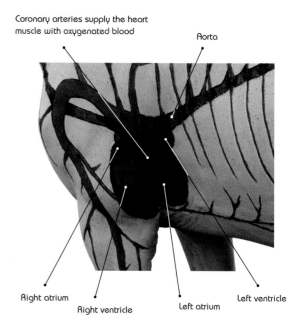

Coronary arteries supply the heart muscle with oxygenated blood

Aorta

Right atrium

Right ventricle

Left atrium

Left ventricle

Pulses

A pulse is a surge of blood pushed through the arteries, powered by the heart. It can be felt at any point where an artery passes over bone close to the skin. Monitoring the strength of the pulse is a useful health indicator. For example a strong throbbing pulse in one medial artery compared to the other leg may indicate a problem in the foot.

The facial artery can be felt on the inner edge of the jawbone.

The lateral and medial palmar digital arteries can be felt just below the fetlock joints.

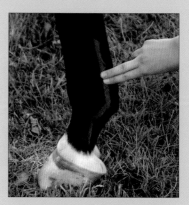

The plantar digital artery can be felt above the fetlock between the suspensory ligament and the back tendons.

CARDIAC RESPONSES TO TRAINING

The horse has an enormous capacity to increase his cardiac output which is the main response to exercise. During maximal exercise the heart rate can rise from 35bpm to 240bpm which is more than six times the resting rate and is more than most other species, including man.

As the heart rate rises, more blood is pumped to the muscles for energy. At rest a fit horse's heart will push one litre of blood into the aorta with each heartbeat. During exercise this can increase to 1.7 litres per heartbeat. As the cardiac muscle pushes more blood around the body blood pressure will increase. This pushes more blood through the capillaries which increase in number providing a greater area for gaseous exchange. This results in greater aerobic efficiency. As the heart strengthens it becomes larger making it easier for the horse to work harder for longer.

Monitoring the heart rate is a useful indication of health and fitness.

Typical Heart Rates after 10 minutes of exercise

Resting heart rate	35–42bpm	This will be lower in a very fit horse
Light work such as walking and trotting	60–150bpm	
Moderate work such as cantering	100–170bpm	Terrain and excitement can affect this
Fast work such as galloping	180 bpm or higher	
Maximal heart rate	240 bpm	
Recovery time after 10–15 minutes of gentle walking	60bpm or lower	In an unfit, excited or dehydrated horse this may take up to 45 minutes.
Fear, pain, stress, infections, injuries and colic can also raise the heart rate.		

In response to stimuli from the sympathetic nervous system, if the horse becomes excited, the heart rate can rise prior to the start of exercise.

The Cardiovascular System

BLOOD VESSELS

Three types of blood vessels carry blood around the body:
1. Arteries
2. Veins
3. Capillaries

The Arteries

Arteries carry bright red oxygenated blood under pressure from the heart to the rest of the body. The one exception is the pulmonary artery, which takes deoxygenated venous blood from the heart to the lungs. As it moves away from the heart, the aorta divides and subdivides reducing in diameter but multiplying in number rather like the branches of a tree. In case of injury, each region of the body is served by several branch systems. The smallest branches are known as arterioles. Under the control of the sympathetic nervous system (see page 116) their function is to regulate blood flow and reduce pressure as blood is transported from the arteries to the capillaries.

Artery walls are made up of thick expandable tissue containing smooth muscle that can withstand the high pressure created by the volume of blood pumped through the arteries by the ventricle pump. If an artery is cut the blood spurts out at the same rate as the pulse. To help reduce this risk most arteries are generally located on the flexor side of a joint or deep within the body. The popliteal and femoral arteries serving the hind leg for example, run behind the stifle joint and in front of the hip respectively.

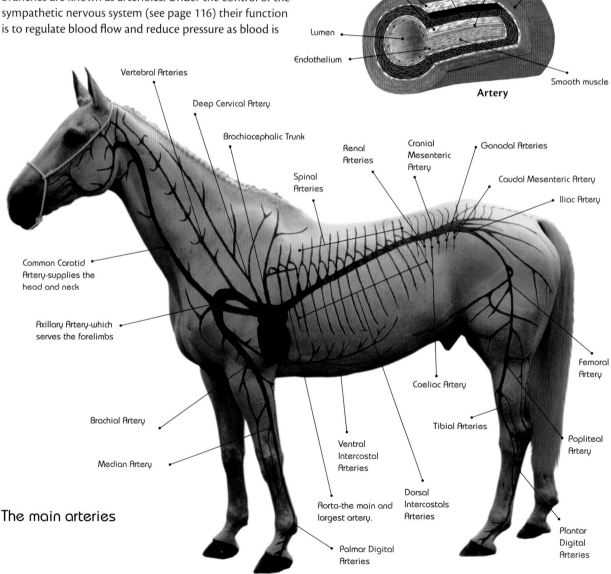

The main arteries

The Veins

Veins transport deoxygenated blood, high in carbon dioxide and waste products, back to the heart. The one exception is the pulmonary vein which carries oxygenated blood from the lungs to the left atrium of the heart. As they do not operate under the same amount of pressure as arteries, the walls are much thinner and valves in the larger veins prevent back flow. If a vein is cut, the escaping blood will be dark red and will not pulse. The smallest veins, the venules, are equivalent to the arterioles in the arterial system. They join together and eventually merge into the vena cava which rejoins the heart at the right atrium.

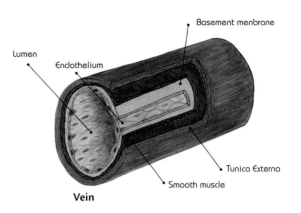

Vein

The main veins follow a similar route to the main arteries

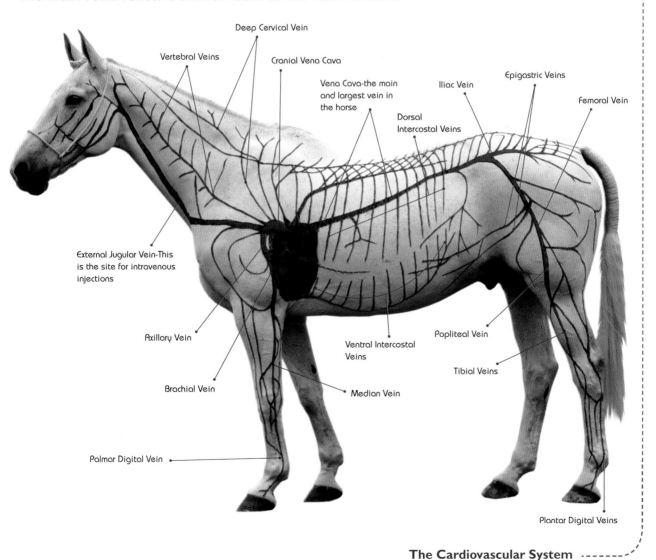

Capillaries

Oxygen and carbon dioxide, as well as minerals and waste materials, are exchanged between blood and cells as the arterialsmeet the venules in the capillaries. With permeable walls and at only one cell thick, these hair like vessels form a lacy network which extends throughout the body. Blood pressure in the capillaries drops to 60% of that in the aorta. This is because rather like a river delta, the area increases and the flow slows.

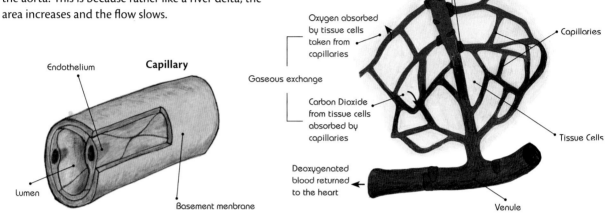

Arteriole

Smooth muscle cells

Smooth muscle cells that act as sphincter muscles to control blood flow through the capillaries. Vascoconstriction

Oxygenated blood from the heart

Oxygen absorbed by tissue cells taken from capillaries

Capillaries

Gaseous exchange

Carbon Dioxide from tissue cells absorbed by capillaries

Tissue Cells

Deoxygenated blood returned to the heart

Venule

Endothelium

Capillary

Lumen

Basement menbrane

Spleen

One third of the horse's red blood cells are stored in the spleen, the position and size of which can vary with respiration and distension of the stomach. As a lymphatic organ, the spleen destroys and removes old and damaged blood cells. The haemoglobin contained in them is broken down and used by the liver to make bile. The iron is recycled to make fresh haemoglobin. The spleen can also produce new red blood cells. The high concentration of red blood cells gives the spleen a dark bluish hue. During exercise these blood cells are released to increase the volume of blood available for gaseous exchange thus increasing the amount of oxygen available to the tissues. This increases stamina and endurance. Thoroughbreds tend to have a larger spleen than crossbred horses. This indicates greater aerobic capacity and athletic potential. Like the human, the horse can function without a spleen. It has been shown that the stamina and performance of horses that have had their spleen removed is very much reduced.

EXERCISE AND THE CARDIOVASCULAR SYSTEM

Understanding the cardiovascular system, knowing how to condition it and how it interrelates with the other systems is crucial to improving performance. It is closely supported by:

1. The respiratory system which provides the oxygen to be circulated to the cells to provide energy (see page 78).
2. The autonomic nervous system which regulates the internal organs including the heart (see page 110).
3. The endocrine system which monitors the blood and regulates flow blood to the internal organs (see page 122).
4. The digestive system which provides the blood with carbohydrates and fats to supply energy to the skeletal muscles (see page 66).
5. The renal system which helps regulate arterial blood pressure (see page 134).

The correct level of cardiac conditioning and fitness is vital for the horse to perform well within his anatomical comfort zone for the sport or activity in which he is required to participate. For optimum performance, the cardiovascular system needs to improve its capacity to deliver oxygen to the working muscles. An unfit horse will tire easily, lose concentration and be more prone to stumbling or hitting a fence.

Respiration

Energy is fuelled by food and provided by a series of chemical reactions between oxygen and glucose from the blood or glycogen from the muscles.

The horse uses two types of respiration when exercising:
1. **Aerobic respiration**. This relies on the delivery of oxygen to the muscle cells via the circulatory system. The by-product, carbon dioxide, attaches to the haemoglobin in the blood, is taken to the lungs and exhaled. Heart rates during aerobic exercise are typically fewer than 150 beats per minute (bpm). Once fit, the horse can sustain this type of exercise for long periods without fatigue. Aerobic exercise strengthens the heart and muscles involved in respiration; improves circulation and the transportation of oxygen in the body, reduces blood pressure, and burns fat. Examples include long-distance work, hacking and dressage.
2. **Anaerobic respiration**. This refers to short duration explosive exercise. It is powered by glycogen taken from the muscles and occurs when the circulatory system cannot work fast enough to transport oxygen to the cells. This type of exercise requires a good aerobic foundation. Anaerobic exercise increases cardiovascular capacity, recovery times, strength, muscle mass and power. The disadvantage is the production of lactic acid which is taken by the blood to the liver for detoxification. A build up of lactic acid can lead to muscle soreness. One way to counteract this is to keep the horse walking for periods of up to an hour to allow the acid to disperse.

To achieve all-round fitness, including endurance, strength, flexibility, power, speed, agility and balance, the horse needs to be worked both aerobically and anaerobically. A combination of the two will build muscle and burn fat. Examples are show jumping courses which incorporate steady canters with explosive jumping efforts and polo which consists of easy canters with sudden accelerations and abrupt stops.

CARDIOVASCULAR FITNESS

Planning a cardiovascular fitness programme is complex, dependent on the age, stage, temperament, breed, discipline and training goal. If in doubt seek the advice of a knowledgeable trainer. A well thought out **individualised programme,** fit for purpose is key to successful training. No matter how fit, a dressage horse would not make a good point to pointer. All fittening work should include some hill work.

- **Long Slow Work (LSW)** forms the basis for endurance and stamina training. It forms the initial stages of all conditioning programmes. For an unbroken, unconditioned horse it can take up to nine months to achieve the desired fitness level. For a previously fit horse coming back from three months at grass it can take 6–10 weeks. Begin with 15 minutes walk work every other day. Gradually increase the workload in increments of 10 minutes progressively introducing trot and canter. LSW also increases the ability to regulate temperature, strengthens bone (see page 18) and increases metabolic activity. LSW can be performed on the lunge, a horse walker or under saddle.

- **Interval Training** improves aerobic capacity by using bursts of faster work separated by short rests to allow the heart rate to lower. Interval training can be used as part of the LSW or the fast work depending on the level of fitness. The aim is to work the horse to raise the heart rate to around 180bpm, walk until the heart rate drops to about 100bpm, then repeat the exercise. A horse aimed at a CCI* event will benefit from three bursts of 5–6 minute canters separated by a short walk of 1–2 minutes. This can be described as stress then rest. As the horse becomes fitter recovery times will diminish.

- **Sprint Training** is high speed conditioning to improve the anaerobic capacity. Racehorses are trained to gallop set distances measured in furlongs. There are eight furlongs in a mile. For a horse aimed at a CCI* as part of a planned programme, event fitness will improve with 2 or 3 sprints up a slightly inclining five furlong gallop no more than every fifth day. This will give the muscles time to recover.

Variety is the Spice of Life!

It is important to include variety in any training programme regardless of discipline. This keeps the horse mentally alert and ensures all muscles are used.

For a fit horse on a maintenance programme this could include:

Day 1 Hack
Day 2 Schooling session – goal orientated
Day 3 Aerobic work out
Day 4 Hack / Interval training
Day 5 Discipline specific schooling session
Day 6 Cross training activity. For example, jumping or pole work for a dressage horse
Day 7 Sprint training
Day 8 Rest day / Walk

Fittening Facts

- The most rapid increase in cardiovascular fitness occurs in the first seven weeks.
- Cardiovascular improvement plateaus after 28 weeks of training.
- It can take up to 12 weeks for the cardio system to return to pre-training fitness levels, depending on the horse and amount of exercise before and during the detraining period.
- After initial training, increased training stimulus will be required to cause an improvement in cardiovascular fitness.
- Maximal heart rate decreases with age. In horses over 20 it can be less than 200bpm.

SUMMARY

- Blood consists of red and white blood cells, plasma and platelets.
- Arteries deliver oxygen-rich blood to the capillaries to be exchanged for carbon dioxide.
- Capillaries deliver the waste-rich blood to the veins for transport back to the heart and lungs.
- The role of the cardiovascular system is to deliver oxygen to the muscles.
- The resting heartbeat of the horse is 35–42 bpm.
- Cardiac output during exercise rises proportionately with workload until maximal heart rates are attained.
- Cardiovascular conditioning reduces the risk of injury and accident.
- An unfit horse, particularly if he is carrying an unfit rider, is more predisposed to injury.
- A fitness programme should be planned in accordance with the end goal.

The Cardiovascular System

The Lymphatic System

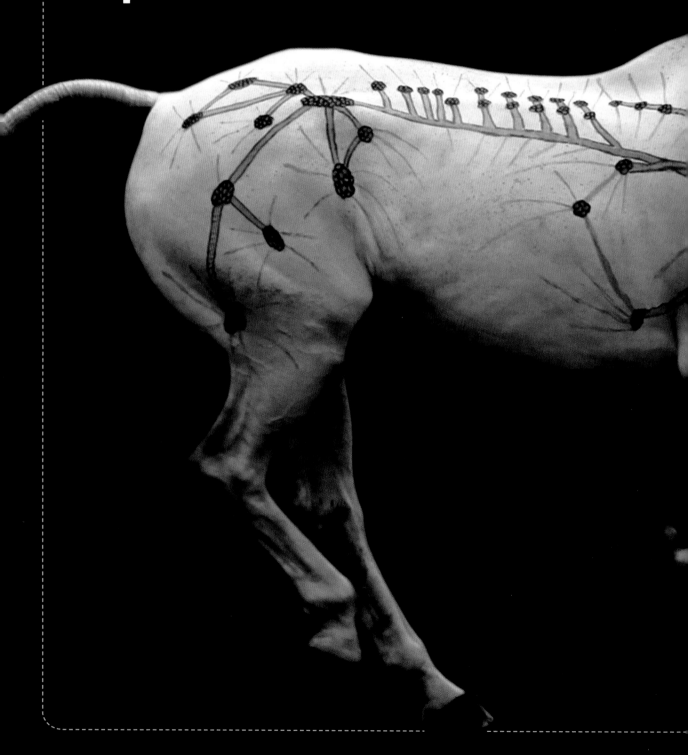

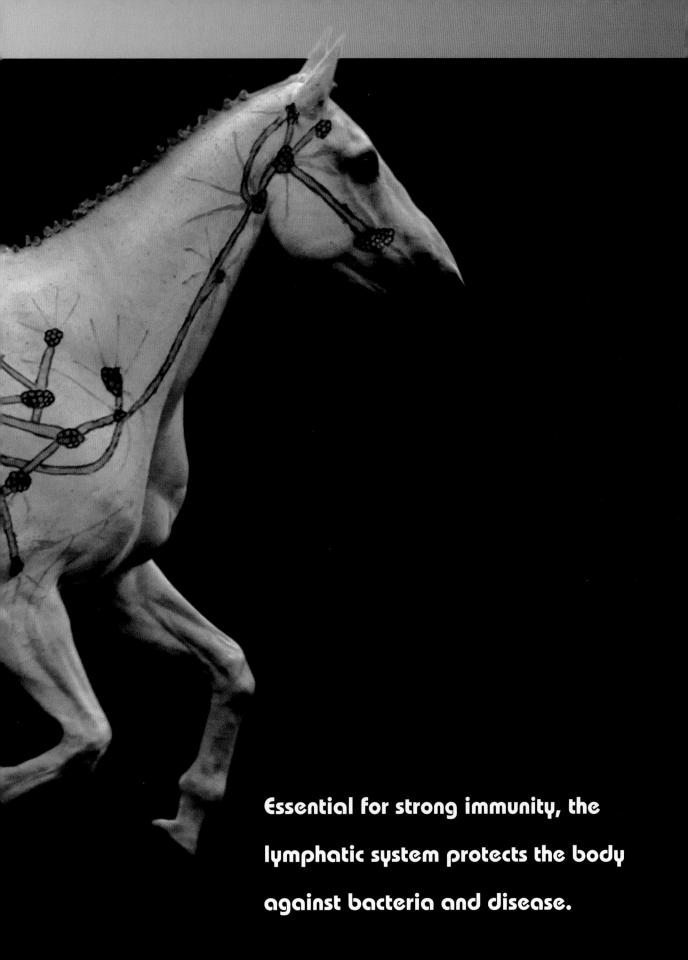

Essential for strong immunity, the lymphatic system protects the body against bacteria and disease.

THE LYMPHATIC SYSTEM

The lymphatic system consists of lymph, lymph vessels, lymph nodes and bone marrow. This system fights infection and is the primary defence against disease and the negative effects of injury. It is therefore an important part of the immune system.

The main functions of the lymphatic system are to:
• fight disease
• maintain a healthy fluid balance by draining excess fluid from the tissues, filtering it and returning it to the blood (see Fluid Balance Facts and Figures).
• cleanse and nourish tissue
• filter bacteria, harmful micro-organisms and toxins in the lymph nodes

• remove waste including damaged, dead or cancerous cells
• assist in the absorption and transport of fats in conjunction with the digestive system (see page 66)
• service, nourish and cleanse the cartilage, cornea and hoof horn which have no blood supply of their own.

The Immune System

The immune system is the body's defence against infectious organisms known as **pathogens.** The lymphatic system produces **lymphocytes**, specialised cells which recognise and destroy pathogens and cancerous cells. As a young horse, who is born with limited immunity, is progressively exposed to specific threats from infection or disease, lymphocytes, which are an essential part of body survival, produce antibodies which remain in the body ready to mount a strong and rapid response should the threat re-emerge.

Immunity is individualised depending on previous exposure to pathogens. This explains why some horses in a yard will succumb to a cough or virus whilst others will remain healthy.

When the immune system becomes weakened through poor diet, stress, dehydration, fatigue, an accumulation of toxins or waste materials or repeated exposure to pathogens, the horse becomes susceptible to illness. Sometimes the immune system becomes hyperactive resulting in a reaction to foreign bodies. Allergies are an example of a hyperactive immune system that over reacts to pollen, dust and other allergens in the environment.

The Spleen

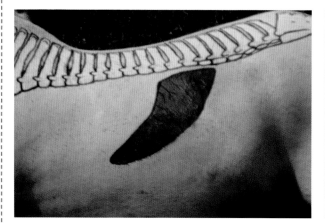

The Thymus

The spleen is the largest mass of lymphatic tissue in the horse's body. Protected within the ribcage, its main function is to produce lymphocytes to fight infection and to remove damaged red blood cells from circulation. It also makes an important contribution to exercise (see page 96).

Lymphocytes are produced by the thymus gland, the spleen and bone marrow. The thymus, situated deep in between the front legs, is also an endocrine gland (see page 126).

Fluid balance facts and figures

- Approximately 70% of the horse's body is water.
- An average horse has 9 gallons of blood.
- 2–3% of the body's fluid is lymph.
- The blood vessels hold about 5% of the horse's total body fluids – a level that is subject to rapid fluctuation as the body's needs change.
- Approximately 15% of the body's water surrounds the blood vessels and cells.
- Up to 50% of the body's water is contained inside the cells.
- 30% of water is stored in the large intestine and caecum, half of which is available to replenish losses elsewhere in the body.

The main Lymphocentres and Lymphatic ducts

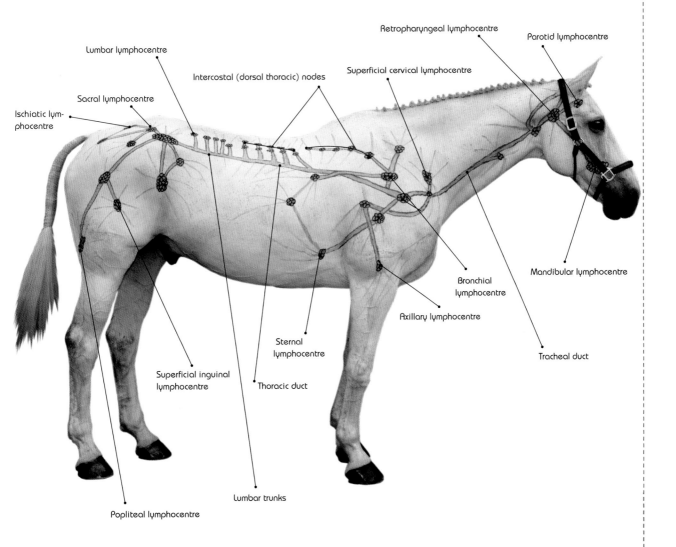

Retropharyngeal lymphocentre

Parotid lymphocentre

Lumbar lymphocentre

Intercostal (dorsal thoracic) nodes

Superficial cervical lymphocentre

Sacral lymphocentre

Ischiatic lymphocentre

Mandibular lymphocentre

Bronchial lymphocentre

Axillary lymphocentre

Tracheal duct

Sternal lymphocentre

Superficial inguinal lymphocentre

Thoracic duct

Lumbar trunks

Popliteal lymphocentre

LYMPH

Unlike the circulatory system, the lymphatic system does not have a central pump. Lymph flow relies primarily on peristalsis and the contraction of skeletal muscle as the horse moves. Valves within the vessels prevent back flow and negative pressure helps to move the lymph upwards into the lymphatic ducts by suction. Inhalation and expiration also contribute to the movement. As the horse breathes the thoracic cavity expands and contracts pulling the lymph towards the heart.

Lymph is a watery, colourless fluid containing lymphocytes, glucose and proteins. It is derived from plasma which seeps from the capillaries to bathe the cells with oxygen and nutrients. Once it has given up its oxygen it drains into the lymphatic capillaries as lymph. This circulates through body tissues picking up fats and bacteria, filtering them out through the lymphatic system. When a horse sustains an injury the clear fluid that oozes from a cut is lymph.

Lymph Vessels

Tiny lymphatic capillaries, only one cell thick, originate in the spaces between the cells. They combine to form a larger network of lymph vessels which intertwine with and follow the same route as the blood capillaries. The lymph vessels join to form the thoracic duct, the main central lymph vessel. This runs under the spine towards the heart. Lymph is returned to the blood close to the heart at the vena cava.

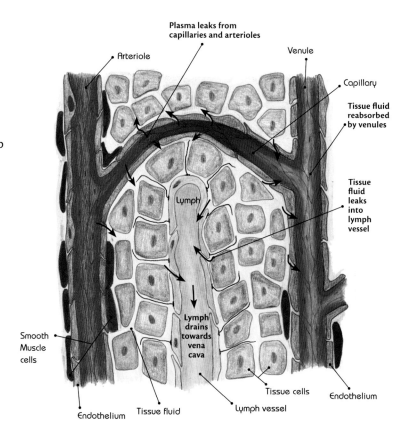

Plasma leaks from capillaries and arterioles

Arteriole

Venule

Capillary

Tissue fluid reabsorbed by venules

Lymph

Tissue fluid leaks into lymph vessel

Smooth Muscle cells

Lymph drains towards vena cava

Tissue cells

Endothelium

Endothelium

Tissue fluid

Lymph vessel

Lymph Nodes

Lymph nodes are groups of small, rounded glands found at intervals along the lymph vessels. They contain disease fighting white blood cells, and produce new disease fighting lymphocytes. These filter out the waste products such as bacteria, debris, dead cells, harmful microbes and toxins which are being transported away from the tissues and destroyed before the lymph returns to the blood stream.

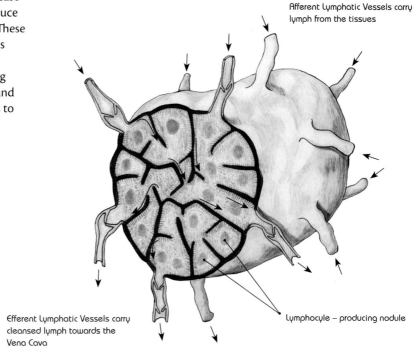

Afferent Lymphatic Vessels carry lymph from the tissues

Efferent Lymphatic Vessels carry cleansed lymph towards the Vena Cava

Lymphocyte – producing nodule

Lymphocentres

These are groups of neighbouring nodes often located close to and responsible for filtrating and cleansing major parts of the body such as the heart, spine, lungs, plexuses, reproductive organs and kidneys. The number of nodes within a group varies. For example, the colic lymph nodes, which are distributed along the length of the colon, are extremely prolific with up to 6,000 nodes!

Lymph vessels

Lymphocentre

Lymph trunk

The Lymphatic System

PRACTICAL APPLICATIONS

When lymph nodes or lymphocentres are actively fighting infection they often swell. This is due to the increased number of lymphocytes recruited to fight the infection.

Sometimes the swellings can be felt particularly in the jaw area. Feeling the parotid, mandibular, sternal and inguinal lymphocentres can be useful in diagnosis. Like ourselves, when the horse is struggling with a virus or infection, he can tire easily and be 'under the weather'. Activity programmes at these times need to be curtailed.

Lymphangitis is an infection of the tissue fluid or lymph. In extreme cases of inactivity the legs may become very hot, swollen and painful. This can also occur as a result of bacterial infection which can be caused by the smallest of cuts, punctures or insect bites. In this situation immediate veterinary intervention is essential.

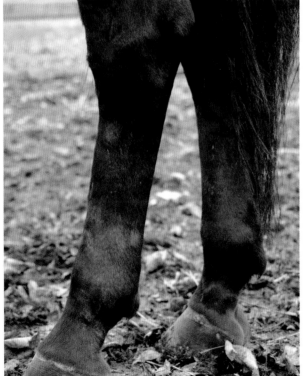

Swelling, or oedema, occurs in circumstances where the lymphatic system cannot rid the tissues of excess fluid. This may be temporary, for example following an injury or because the lymphatic system itself fails. This condition is known as lymphoedema. With no muscles below the knee and hock, and in the absence of a pump, inactivity, lack of sufficient exercise or space in which to move can cause the legs to fill as lymph accumulates in the tissues and joints. This can be a problem for a horse on box rest. Bandaging the legs is not the answer. The fluid will disperse once activity is resumed. Manual lymph drainage massage techniques can sometimes be helpful in reducing lymphoedema.

During exercise there is an increase in toxins and waste products as a result of micro trauma and increased respiration. There is also increased hormonal activity linked to stress and travelling. The lymphatic system plays an important role in cleansing muscle tissue and helping it to recover. Although this cleansing process starts during exercise, it may take several hours to complete. To keep the lymph flowing, as well as allowing the heart and respiration rate to return to normal, it is important to keep the horse gently moving for up to two hours after strenuous exercise.

This yellow triangle is the most common site for injecting intramuscular medicines which are filtered into the blood stream via the lymph.

SUMMARY

- The main function of the lymphatic system is to fight disease.
- Lymph is a colourless fluid, derived from the blood, which helps fight infection.
- Lymph is moved round the body by the muscles.
- Lymph regulates, redistributes and adjusts fluid balance.
- The thymus, bone marrow and spleen produce lymphocytes which destroy pathogens.
- When the horse is fighting infection, the lymph nodes swell and can be felt beneath the skin.
- Inactivity can cause the legs to swell.

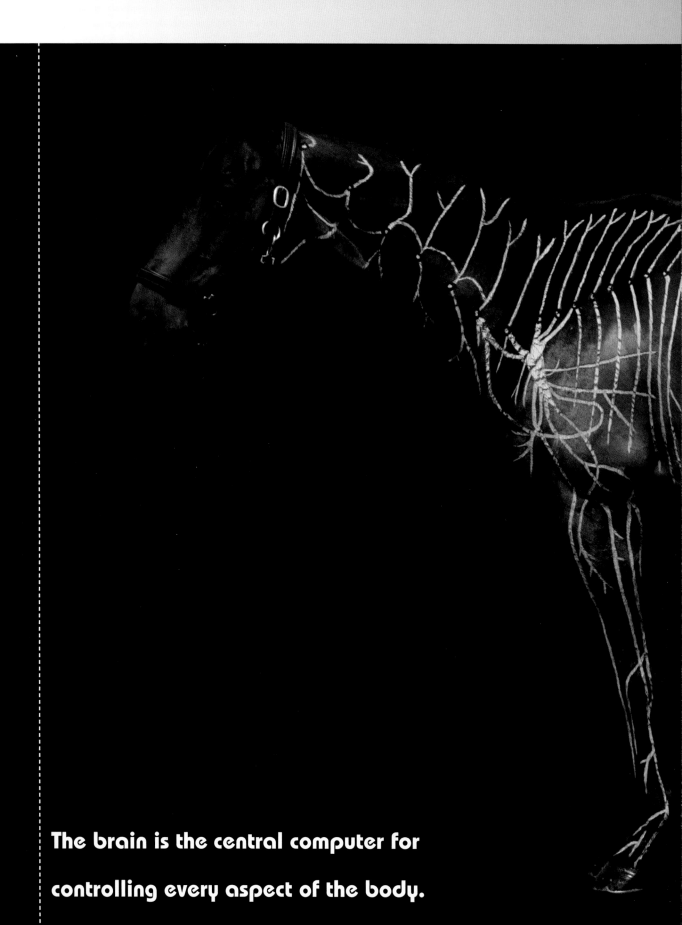

The brain is the central computer for controlling every aspect of the body.

The Nervous System

A SYSTEM OF COMMUNICATION

The nervous system is the most complex in the body. Made up of the brain, spinal cord and an intricate network of nerves, operating through high speed nerve impulses, it co-ordinates all the other systems and initiates all voluntary movements. It controls actions, reactions, reflexes, the senses, movement, feeling, behaviour, activity, all responses to the environment, training and involuntary movements such as heartbeat, breathing and digestion. The nervous system is subdivided into two systems which constantly communicate and interact with each other.

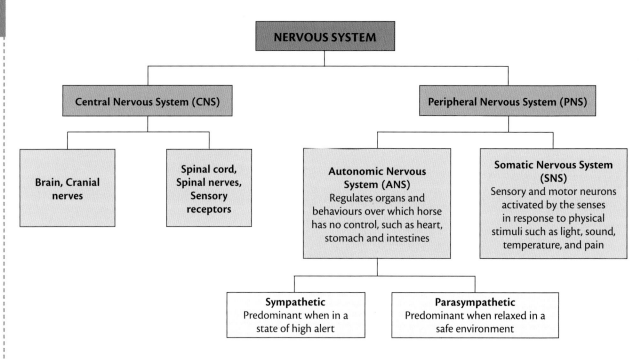

NERVOUS SYSTEM

Central Nervous System (CNS)

- **Brain, Cranial nerves**
- **Spinal cord, Spinal nerves, Sensory receptors**

Peripheral Nervous System (PNS)

- **Autonomic Nervous System (ANS)** Regulates organs and behaviours over which horse has no control, such as heart, stomach and intestines
- **Somatic Nervous System (SNS)** Sensory and motor neurons activated by the senses in response to physical stimuli such as light, sound, temperature, and pain

- **Sympathetic** Predominant when in a state of high alert
- **Parasympathetic** Predominant when relaxed in a safe environment

The Reflex Arc

Reflexes, rapid involuntary responses to stimuli, are often protective. For example, a horse blinks to shield the eye and will respond to a troublesome fly by twitching the skin. The reflex arc comes into play when immediate action is required. To avoid injury and allow immediate withdrawal from a dangerous situation, nerve endings, responsive to pain, temperature, pressure and touch, send massages directly to the spinal cord which then sends an immediate signal via motor neurons to the muscle to react.

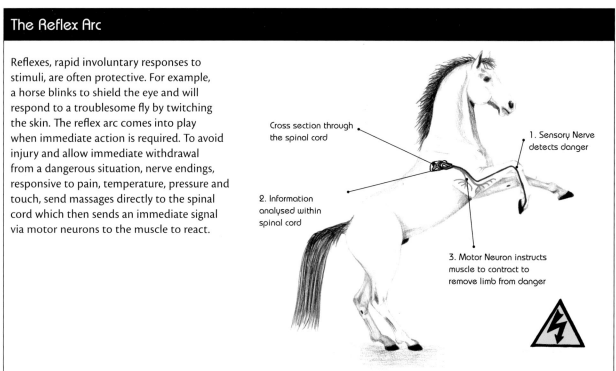

Cross section through the spinal cord

1. Sensory Nerve detects danger

2. Information analysed within spinal cord

3. Motor Neuron instructs muscle to contract to remove limb from danger

Nerves and Neurons

The nervous system is composed from vast numbers of cells known as neurons. Bundled together they specialise in carrying messages around the body. They respond to all types of stimuli and can be likened to telephone wires sending messages to a central computer.

The structure of all neurons, the basic units of the nervous system, is similar although they do vary in size, shape, location and function. A foal is born with its full complement. Each neuron has three parts: the cell body, axon and dentrites.

There are three types of neuron:

- **Sensory neurons** which generally have long dendrites to carry messages from the senses to the CNS.
- **Motor neurons** which have one long axon and short dendrites, carry messages from the brain to the muscles and glands in all parts of the body.
- **Interneurons** send information between sensory and motor neurons and are found only in the CNS.

Nerve impulses are initiated in sensory receptors in every part of the body. The receptors are responsive to stimuli such as touch, pressure, sound, stretch, motion and

When the rider's heel touches the horse's skin, pressure receptors transmit the information to the brain for interpretation.

many more. The neurons, which do not actually touch, are separated by junctions known as **synapses**. Electrical impulses are sent along the neuron dendrites and axons. At a synapse, the nerve impulse is carried across the gap by a chemical known as a neurotransmitter which binds to a specialised docking area on the adjacent cell known as a receptor. Nerve impulses travel in a few milliseconds which allows for an almost instantaneous response to stimuli. When a neural pathway is used regularly and repeatedly, the number of neurotransmitters and receptors increase making movement more natural and easier to perform. Conversely, when a movement is not performed regularly, neurotransmitters and receptors decrease and fluency of movement is lost.

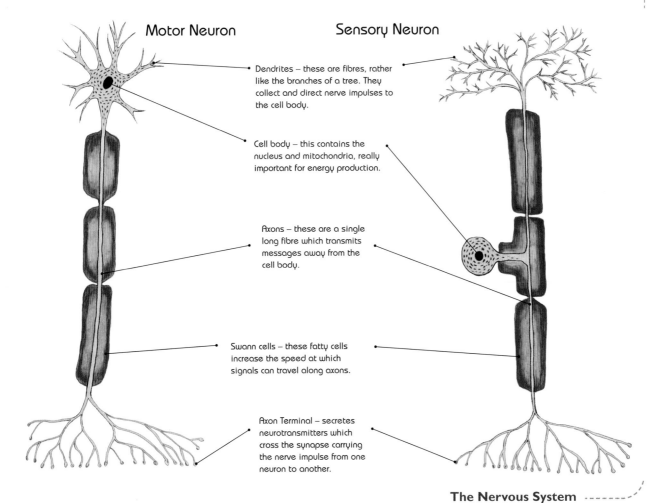

Motor Neuron

Sensory Neuron

Dendrites – these are fibres, rather like the branches of a tree. They collect and direct nerve impulses to the cell body.

Cell body – this contains the nucleus and mitochondria, really important for energy production.

Axons – these are a single long fibre which transmits messages away from the cell body.

Swann cells – these fatty cells increase the speed at which signals can travel along axons.

Axon Terminal – secretes neurotransmitters which cross the synapse carrying the nerve impulse from one neuron to another.

The Nervous System

THE CENTRAL NERVOUS SYSTEM

The brain and spinal cord form the centre of the nervous system. Protected by the cranium, surrounded by cerebral fluid and encased by the meninges, a protective, nourishing membrane, they control the other systems either by activating muscles or by causing secretion of chemicals such as neurotransmitters and hormones (see page 124). This centralised control allows rapid and co-ordinated responses to changes in the environment. The brain uses 20% of the oxygen inhaled into the lungs.

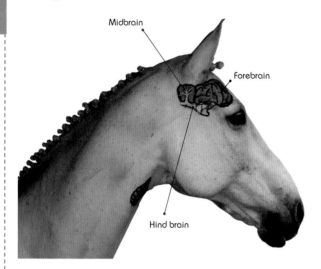

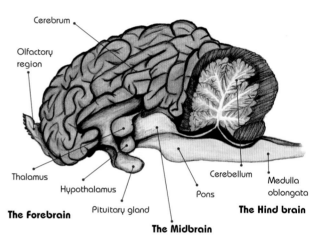

The Forebrain

The Midbrain

The Hind brain

The Brain

The brain in the horse is relatively small. It accounts for about 0.1% of the body and weighs an average of 0.6kg. It is divided into three main segments, each of which is associated with but not exclusively responsible for specialised functions.

1. The Forebrain accounts for 75% of the total volume. It is subdivided into 4 regions:

- **The Cerebrum** – the largest area of the brain is ridged and furrowed to accommodate the hundreds of thousands of neurons and their fibres which connect different parts of the brain. Drawing on past memories it reacts to sensations such as vision, hearing, temperature, touch and smell (see page 81), controls and co-ordinates most physical and mental activities and is the centre for learning, disposition, mood, emotion and intelligence.
- **The Hypothalamus** – forms the base of the forebrain and is about the size of a grape. It is connected by a stalk to the pituitary gland. It controls the glands of the endocrine system (see page 122) and the autonomic nervous system over which the horse has no control. This includes regulating blood pressure and temperature, behavioural and sexual responses, aggression and pleasure.

- **The Thalamus** – responsible for initial sorting of incoming messages and directing them to the appropriate areas of the brain for processing.
- The Olfactory Lobe – concerned with the sense of smell.

2. The Midbrain, situated behind the cerebrum, controls responses to sensations of sight and smell as well as the voluntary control of breathing, behaviour and movement.

3. The Hindbrain
- **The Medulla Oblongata** – links the spinal chord and brain and controls the vital processes such as heartbeat, digestion, respiration and breathing. It also co-ordinates swallowing, coughing and sneezing.
- **The Cerebellum** – also known as the little brain, is rather like a smaller version of the cerebrum responsible for controlling balance, posture, movement and muscular activity.
- **The Pons** – links the medulla oblongata and thalamus in the right and left hemispheres.

The Spinal Cord

The spinal cord, housed within the vertebral column, comprises of a long rope of nerve fibres carrying messages between the brain and every other part of the body. Approximately 200 centimetres in length it runs from the medulla oblongata to the middle of the sacrum. 8 cervical, 18 thoracic, 6 lumbar, 5 sacral and 5 coccygeal nerves emerge from between the vertebral bodies. The diameter of the spinal cord, about 2–3cm, is greatest in the cervical and lumbar vertebral bodies from where the nerves supplying the limbs emerge.

Cross-Section of the Spinal Cord

The spinal cord consists of grey matter, which contains the nerve cell bodies, and white matter which contains axons travelling long distances to the brain. Each sensory dorsal root joins with a motor ventral root to form a spinal nerve. The dura mater, the outer most meninx, is a tough fibrous tissue covering the spinal cord.

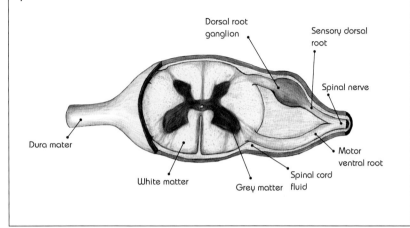

Dorsal root ganglion

Sensory dorsal root

Spinal nerve

Dura mater

Motor ventral root

White matter

Grey matter

Spinal cord fluid

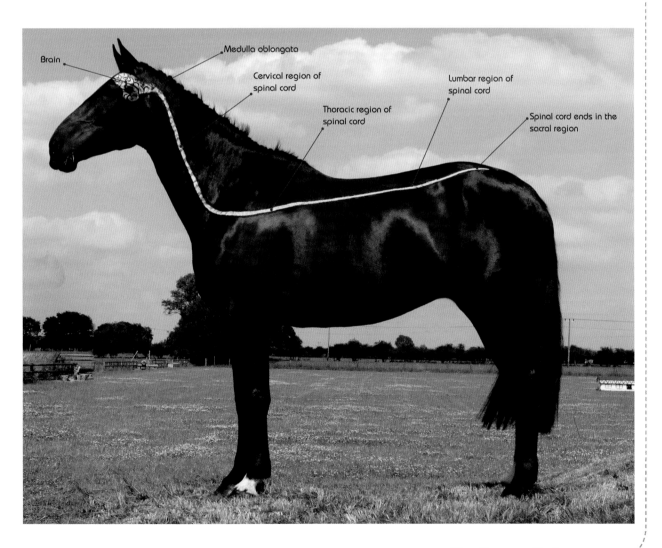

Brain

Medulla oblongata

Cervical region of spinal cord

Thoracic region of spinal cord

Lumbar region of spinal cord

Spinal cord ends in the sacral region

PERIPHERAL NERVOUS SYSTEM

On emerging from between the vertebrae, the spinal nerves divide into two branches. The dorsal branches supply the skin, muscles, bones and fascia above the spinal cord and the larger ventral branches supply the limbs and those below.

Running over the scalene muscle and lying under the shoulder joint for protection, the brachial plexus, a web of cervical and thoracic ventral nerve branches serve the flexor and extensor muscles of the forelimb. An injury here is serious and may cause a positional abnormality, muscle atrophy, the inability to bear weight and extend or flex the forelimb.

The lumbosacral plexus serves the hind limb. This is a hub of ventral branches of the lumbar and sacral nerves. These penetrate the abdominal roof wall and the pelvic cavity. They run deep within the body well protected under the spine, pelvis and between the femurs.

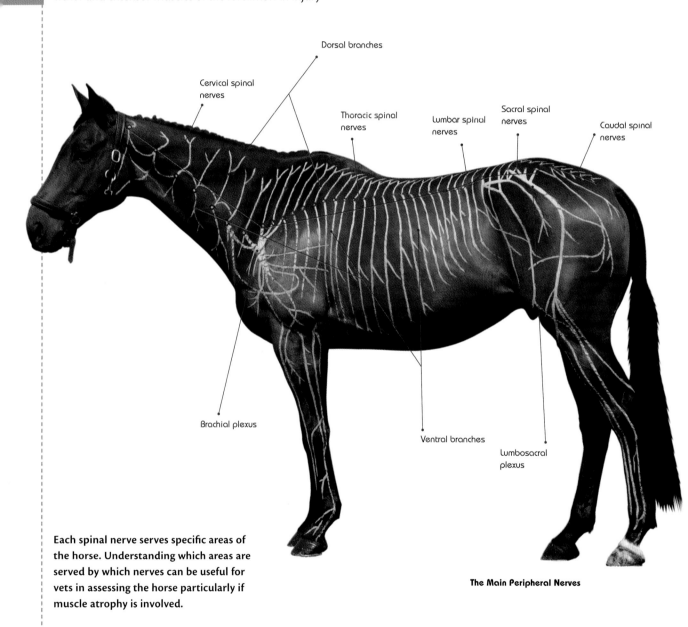

The Main Peripheral Nerves

Each spinal nerve serves specific areas of the horse. Understanding which areas are served by which nerves can be useful for vets in assessing the horse particularly if muscle atrophy is involved.

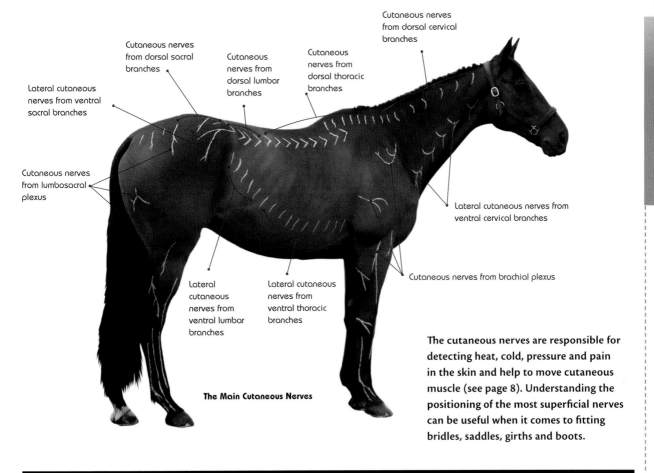

Cutaneous nerves from dorsal cervical branches

Cutaneous nerves from dorsal sacral branches

Cutaneous nerves from dorsal lumbar branches

Cutaneous nerves from dorsal thoracic branches

Lateral cutaneous nerves from ventral sacral branches

Cutaneous nerves from lumbosacral plexus

Lateral cutaneous nerves from ventral cervical branches

Lateral cutaneous nerves from ventral lumbar branches

Lateral cutaneous nerves from ventral thoracic branches

Cutaneous nerves from brachial plexus

The Main Cutaneous Nerves

The cutaneous nerves are responsible for detecting heat, cold, pressure and pain in the skin and help to move cutaneous muscle (see page 8). Understanding the positioning of the most superficial nerves can be useful when it comes to fitting bridles, saddles, girths and boots.

Dermatones

A dermatome is a surface area of the body served by a specific nerve or group of nerves. Although each dermatome covers roughly the same area they do vary from horse to horse. Pain can be referred to areas of the body anywhere along the route of the nerve serving the site of pain. For example, damage to a nerve in the lumbar region could be referred along the ventral branch of the first lumbar nerve and present as pain above the stifle in its associate dermatome. This can sometimes make diagnosing a problem challenging.

The peripheral nervous system can be subdivided into the:

- **Somatic or voluntary nervous system.** This brings signals from the external sense receptors to the brain which responds by sending signals known as **effectors** to the muscles to act appropriately.
- **Autonomic nervous system (ANS).** This consists of motor neurons that control cardiac and smooth muscles in the internal organs such as the intestine, bladder and uterus. Organs are supplied by nerves from two subdivisions of the ANS which work in opposition to each other.
  1. **The Sympathetic Nervous System** is involved in the fight or flight response. It raises awareness of the senses, increases the capacity of the circulatory and respiratory systems and suppresses the digestive system. It increases sweating, heartbeat and blood flow, dilates pupils, and inhibits bodily functions such as salivation or urination.
  2. **The Parasympathetic Nervous System** is in action when the horse is in a safe, relaxed environment. It slows heartbeat, increases salivation and allows urination.

Understanding the ANS can alert riders to the psychological state of the horse.

When the horse is scared, the somatic nervous system comes into play. Horses with different temperaments respond differently to perceived fear. For example in a scary situation, one horse may bolt whilst another may just step aside. Responses to pain or fear can include backing away, lunging sideways or in extreme cases bucking, rearing, kicking or biting. As the anatomy of the brain does not allow the horse to premeditate his actions, these responses are borne of instinctive self preservation rather than vicious intent.

In a relaxed environment the parasympathetic nervous system will be predominant. Understanding the autonomic nervous system is useful in handling and training. Creating a calm environment, patience, gentle handling and reassuring tones elicit desired behaviours and encourage parasympathetic responses. New lessons should be introduced slowly without over pressurising the horse. Loud aggressive tones, impatience and rough handling stimulate sympathetic behaviours which stimulate fight flight response and inhibit learning. Some horses with an enlarged amygdala, the area of the brain involved in emotional processing, are more highly strung, and although they require more patience and understanding during training, they often make good competition horses as they respond to excitement by releasing more adrenalin.

Horse Behaviour Fight or Flight?

As a prey and herd animal, horses have developed survival mechanisms for protection. Although real threats no longer exist for the domesticated horse, the primitive instinct to survive and to escape from perceived danger remains. The frontal lobes of the brain, responsible for thinking and analysing, are much reduced in the horse. When he is faced with a potentially dangerous situation, the first brain structure to become activated is the amygdala, closely followed by the hypothalamus, which sanctions the release of the hormone adrenalin. This causes the pupils to dilate, the heartbeat to quicken and blood pressure to increase. With heightened awareness the horse is now ready for flight. This is the sympathetic nervous system in action. Once the perceived danger has passed the parasympathetic nervous system is activated to calm and relax.

THE SENSES

The horse uses his somatic senses, including pain, temperature and pressure together with sight, hearing, touch, taste and smell to make sense of his environment and feed information to the nervous system. Understanding how they function can shed light on some behavioural traits.

Sight

The horse has the largest eyes of any land mammal. He has almost panoramic vision.

• Monocular vision enables him to see different things with each eye. This allows him to see and be startled by something in a hedge without turning his head.
• Binocular vision involves both eyes and enables him to focus on objects directly in front of him. The horse uses positioning of his head and neck to maximise his vision. To focus on a jump he needs to lift his head. When the neck is overbent, the horse can only see his feet.

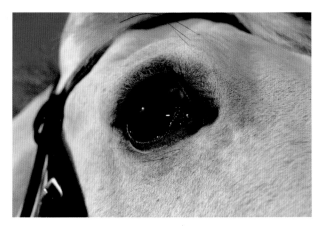

Unlike humans who have a spherical eyeball, that of the horse is slightly flattened. The retina is closer to the lens at the bottom of the eye than the top. This means that when grazing, the retina is able to focus both on the grass and the distance and explains why when being approached in a field he can eat and keep his eye on a person or another horse.

The eye works in a similar fashion to a camera. The cornea, a protective coating covering the iris and pupil, together with the lens refracts the light, assists in focussing and then projects an inverted image onto the retina at the back of the eye. This contains millions of light sensitive cells known as photoreceptors. Light sensitive rods allow the horse to see in a dim light whilst colour sensitive cones decipher colour. The photoreceptors create nerve impulses which are sent to the brain for interpretation via the optic nerve.

Hearing

Sound waves travel as vibrations in the air and are picked up by the large mobile external ears which can be used independently rather like antennae. As well as directing sound, they also indicate emotion. Often when being ridden, one ear is directed towards the rider. This indicates concentration. If the ears are pricked the horse is alert. If they fall sideways they indicate relaxation and if flat back indicate aggression.

Sound is funnelled down the auditory canal to the eardrum. Sound waves strike this thin membrane causing it to vibrate. The vibrations are then directed towards three bones in the middle ear which are collectively known as the ossicles. Sound waves cause the first bone, the hammer, to hit the second bone, the anvil, which in turn strikes the stirrup, the smallest bone in the body. This amplifies the sound waves and sends them into the inner ear. Canals known as eustachian tubes connect the middle ear to the throat and ensure an even pressure is maintained in the ear. Within the inner ear is the cochlea. This small snail shaped, liquid filled chamber is the start of the auditory nerve. Thousands of tiny hairs carry the sound waves along the nerve to be decoded by the brain.

A highly developed sense of hearing, well outside the human range, allows the horse to monitor the world around him. Horses hear higher pitched sounds than people and will often stand listening in a stance of heightened awareness.

Taste and Smell

The sense of smell is highly developed and used not only to detect foods but also other horses, people and prospective mates, all as part of a complicated social structure. Horses frequently greet each other nose to nose recognising them by scent as well as sight. They are often seen standing erect sniffing the air or sniffing droppings in a field. Horses greet people in the same way, sniffing the hand to take in the pheromones. To familiarise and memorise new scents, horses raise their head and curl their lip in the flehman posture (see page 81).

The chemical sense of taste and smell are very closely linked. By smelling, the horse avoids unpalatable or harmful foods. This explains why he will not drink tainted water or eat unpleasant medicines however carefully they are disguised. Food is mixed with saliva which dissolves the chemicals. Taste buds, located on the tongue and soft palate, distinguish between sweet, bitter, sharp and salty foods. Some food molecules find their way into the nose. Turbinate bones at the back of the nasal chamber secrete mucous in which the olfactory cells which send signals to the brain for processing are situated.

Touch

The physical sensations of touch, pressure, pain, heat and cold are detected by specialised sensory receptors located in the skin (see page 6). Sensitivity varies according to thickness of the skin, coat, breed, age and the number of receptors. Thoroughbreds tend to have a thinner more delicate skin than a cob. This means they feel the cold more readily. The area around the eyes, lips and nose are particularly receptor dense. With whiskers that relay additional sensory information, the muzzle is acutely sensitive.

Much training is accomplished through the sense of touch sending signals to the brain through the rider's legs, seat and hands. The horse is capable of detecting the most subtle of aids. He can, after all, detect a fly on his coat! If harsh training methods are used whereby the rider continually pulls at the mouth or kicks at the ribs, the horse will become desensitised and less responsive.

The nostrils are surrounded by a strong ring of cartilage which can dilate to take in more air and intensify the sense of smell.

Touching plays an important part in communication, not only in courtship and between mare and foal, but also with mutual grooming and bonding between horse and human. Rewarding or calming the horse by gentle stroking rewards him for a job well done, reinforces learning and gives him a sense of relaxation.

THERAPIES AND THE NERVOUS SYSTEM

Both the autonomic and somatic nervous systems can be influenced by physical therapy.

Effleurage, a gentle stroke massage technique stimulates the touch receptors in the skin. It also stimulates a natural opiate release, reducing the sensation of pain and promoting general relaxation.

Passive stretching and movements stimulate the stretch receptors and proprioception in the joints. This is particularly good for horses on box rest.

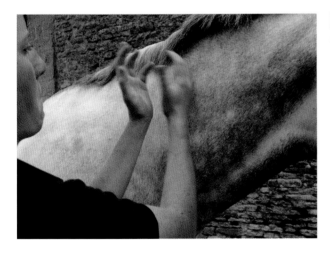

The continuous, repetitive, rhythmical stimuli of **tapotement** or **strapping** warms and stimulates the circulation. This is useful as part of a daily grooming routine.

Petrissage is a technique similar to kneading bread. It mobilises muscle and fascia, influences pressure receptors in the superficial tissues and influences the movement of venous blood and lymph.

PRACTICAL APPLICATION

The central nervous system (CNS) plays an important role in exercise training as it determines the amount of blood sent to the working muscles. It is also involved in mechanical efficiency. Some adaptations and improvements are evident after 2–4 schooling sessions, but generally improvements are consolidated in 2–6 weeks. Peripheral adaptations can take 6–12 months.

Movement, Balance and Proprioception

Proprioception is the spatial awareness that allows the horse to unconsciously monitor the position of his body and co-ordinate balance and movement. It is part of the Vestibular System which is primarily concerned with balance, co-ordination and agility. Proprioceptors consist of sensory and motor nerves situated in muscles, tendons, ligaments and joints that send messages to and from the central nervous system to adjust posture and movement. The unconscious perception of body parts in relation to each other and the environment enables the horse to develop the expression of the dressage horse and the agility of a jumper.

Proprioception can be enhanced by both in hand and ridden exercises. Lateral work, walking over and between poles, passive stretching, turn about the forehand, hill work and gymnastic jumping all improve body awareness and encourage the horse to be co-ordinated, balanced and relaxed.

Proprioception is enhanced if the horse is:
• calm and relaxed
• warm. Increased body temperature speeds the interaction between nerve impulses and the receptors in nerves, tendons and muscles. This is an important reason for a structured warm up.

Proprioception is reduced if the horse is:
• cold
• stressed or excited. In this state he is less aware of his body and more likely to perform badly, tripping or knocking down a pole when showjumping
• fatigued.

Horses that live and work on a steep hillside and are ridden over a variety of terrain have increased neural stimulation and greater proprioception than those living in a stable and being trained solely on a pristine surface.

Although the nervous system cannot be conditioned in the same way as the respiratory or cardiovascular systems, speed of reaction increases with repetition. This is because the number of neural pathways together with the speed of nerve impulses and neurotransmission at synapses increase with use. This is the science behind the old adage, 'practice makes perfect!' The more times the horse trots over the poles, the more proficient he will become until the movement is imprinted and becomes second nature. It is then a learned movement pattern. Rather like riding a bike, once learned never forgotten!

EXERCISE AND TRAINING OF THE NERVOUS SYSTEM

Conditioning

A calm relaxed atmosphere combined with patience, consistency and repetition is conducive to learning and provides an optimum environment for the function of the nervous system whatever the task, age or stage.

Rehabilitation from Injury

Horses like people respond to pain by developing compensatory movement patterns. As an avoidance strategy for pain, the horse will forge new neural pathways within the musculoskeletal system which, once established, may be difficult to break. The horse has a long memory and once the initial injury is repaired the compensatory movement pattern may linger. To avoid this scenario it is important to get the horse moving comfortably and normally as soon as possible before the new movement pattern becomes established.

Exercises incorporating changes of speed and direction train the horse to be mentally alert, responsive and quick thinking. Jumping fences at different speeds and angles keeps him focussed and helps to improve reactions.

Some learned movement patterns or imprinted responses are unhelpful. For example if a young horse is always led from the left, he will associate pressure on the nose with turning his head to the left. This can be an unwelcome response as he comes into training. Avoiding a bad habit is better than trying to break it!

SUMMARY

- The CNS is made up of the brain and spinal chord.
- It controls all actions, reactions and behaviours.
- The neuron forms the base unit of the nervous system.
- Nerves carry messages from the brain to the muscles and organs.
- The brain accounts for 0.1% body weight.
- Information is gathered through the senses.
- The fight flight instinct remains strong in the domesticated horse.
- Horses do not have the brain capacity to plan or think ahead. They can only respond to situations.
- The nervous system responds well to physical therapies.
- A calm disposition, repetition and consistency of aids are key to successful training.

The Endocrine System

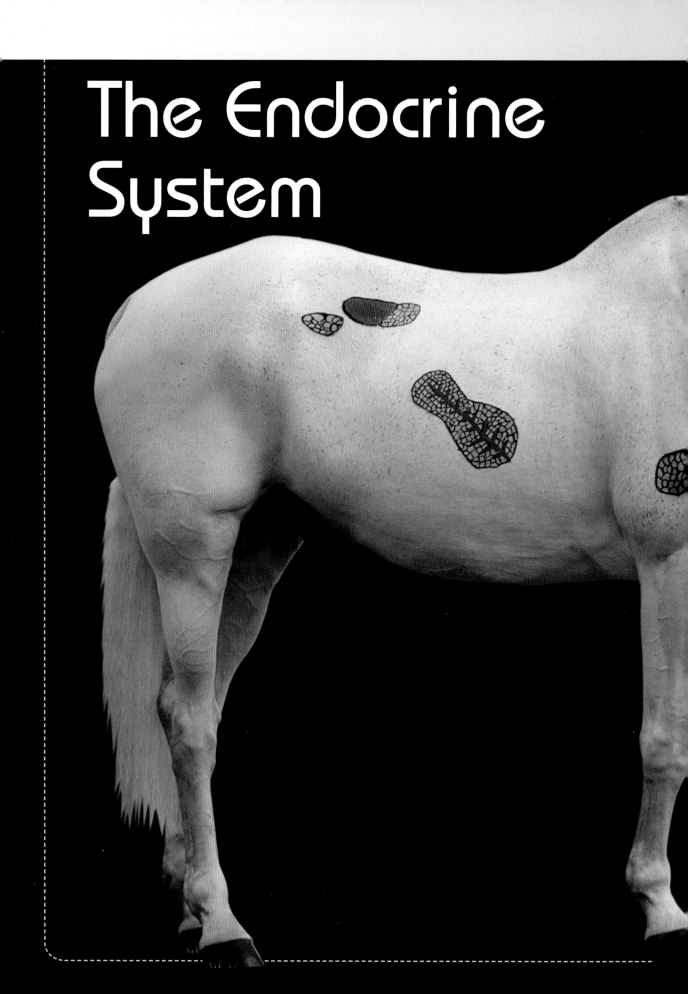

Hormones, secreted by the endocrine system, are the chemical messengers that regulate growth, reproduction, digestion and every other function of the body.

THE ENDOCRINE SYSTEM COMPARED TO THE NERVOUS SYSTEM

The endocrine system works closely with the nervous system to maintain stability and transmit messages around the body. Both are systems of communication. Whereas the nervous system (see page 108) controls actions and reactions via rapid electrical impulses, the endocrine, a much slower method of communication, uses chemical messengers known as hormones secreted from a series of glands. These are carried in the blood or lymph to other parts of the body where they help control the function of cells and target organs.

Endocrine System	Nervous System
• Method of internal communication • Sends slower chemical messages • Hormones carry messages in the blood • Effects are longer lasting • Glands secrete hormones • Often regulated by the hypothalamus • Some hormones stimulate nerves	• Method of internal communication • Sends rapid electrical messages • Nervous messages transmitted directly from neuron to neuron • Effects are short lived • Neurones secrete neurotransmitters • Regulated by the central nervous system • Information from the senses analysed by the hypothalamus • Some neurons stimulate endocrine glands

Endocrine Function

Functions controlled by the Endocrine System include:
- Growth
- Digestion
- Emotion
- Reproduction
- Immune responses
- Behaviour
- Metabolism
- Development

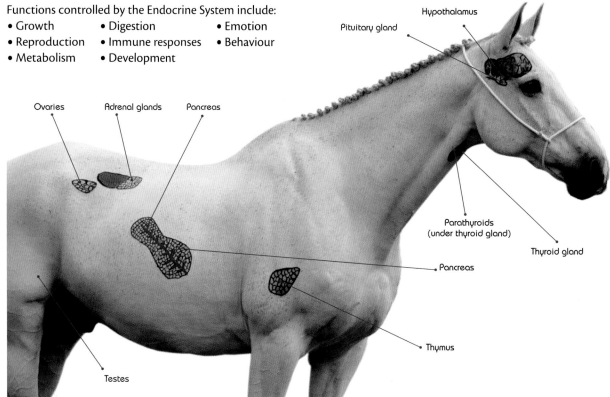

Hypothalamus

Pituitary gland

Ovaries   Adrenal glands   Pancreas

Parathyroids (under thyroid gland)

Thyroid gland

Pancreas

Thymus

Testes

Hormones and the Metabolism

A **hormone** is a naturally occurring substance secreted by specialised glands that adjusts body metabolism.

Metabolism is the rate at which the body burns calories for energy.

The **Metabolic rate** is the speed of metabolism.

If a horse is bitten by a horse fly, the nervous system responds. If a stallion sees a mare, the endocrine system responds.

HYPOTHALAMUS

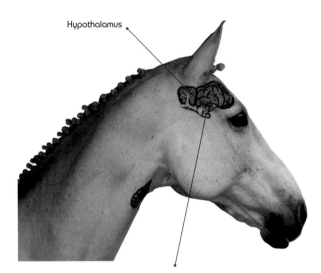

Hypothalamus

Pituitary gland

Some of the main functions of the hypothalamus are to:
- control and regulate hormones released from the pituitary gland
- maintain the equilibrium of the body including heartbeat, digestion, liver and kidney function, urination and defecation
- regulate body temperature (see page 12)
- control blood pressure
- maintain fluid and electrolyte balance
- regulate appetite and metabolism
- control sexual behaviour.

The hypothalamus, itself an endocrine gland, is the main link between the endocrine and nervous systems. It deciphers and co-ordinates signals sent from the external environment via the senses and decodes feedback sent from the internal organs. Messages are then sent to the nervous or endocrine systems as appropriate.

The hypothylamus influences emotional reactions such as anger, aggression and pleasure.

The Endocrine System

PITUITARY GLAND

Often referred to as the master gland, the pituitary controls several other endocrine glands producing:

- **Growth Hormones**. Vigorous sustained anaerobic exercise encourages the production of growth hormones, which:
  - help strengthen bones, ligaments, tendons and cartilage
  - encourage the use of fats for energy
  - help balance blood glucose levels and allow the horse to be trained over a longer period of time
  - boost energy and the ability to concentrate
  - increase aerobic capacity and strength.
- **Endorphins** are neurotransmitters that inhibit feelings of pain and activate opiate receptors, which engender euphoria and relaxation. Prolonged exercise boosts production and enhances the feel good factor as does deep tissue massage. Chewing, a natural behaviour, has also been linked to endorphin release. Horses left without food may resort to crib biting, an addictive behaviour which may bring a pleasurable calming effect. Once established, due to positive feedback, this trait is difficult to eliminate.
- **Antidiuretic hormones** which help control water balance and urine output through their effect on the kidneys.
- **Various other sex hormones** which influence the testes, ovaries, labour and milk production in mares (see page 129).

Pituitary Gland Problems

The most common pituitary gland dysfunction is known as Cushing's. This syndrome is caused by a benign tumour of the pituitary leading to overproduction of cortisol from the adrenal gland. This results in increased blood glucose levels. The main clinical manifestations of this hormonal imbalance are:
- a long curly coat
- repeated laminitis and associated hoof abscesses
- excessive sweating
- chronic infections
- increased water consumption and urination
- lethargy
- loss of muscle particularly in the back and hindquarters
- enlarged abdomen.

Although the various symptoms can be managed in the early stages, there is no cure.

Electrolytes

The hypothalamus and pituitary glands are both involved in metabolising electrolytes. During exercise a horse can lose up to 10 litres of sweat in two hours. This can dramatically increase during heavy work or in hot, humid conditions. Loss of salts such as potassium and sodium chloride can result in tiredness, muscle stiffness, dehydration and sometimes colic. Following strenuous exercise the horse should be rehydrated with water and electrolytes should be added to feed to replace lost salts. This will improve performance and aid recovery.

THYMUS

This two-lobed gland is located between the lungs and in the foal it can reach up the neck as far as the thyroid. Its main function is to fight disease and produce specialised lymphocytes which target and destroy invading microbes, tumours and cancerous cells. It is particularly important during gestation and as a foal to help develop immunity and to protect against infection. Once the foal reaches maturity the thymus starts to recede and become relatively inactive. It is also part of the lymphatic system (see page 100).

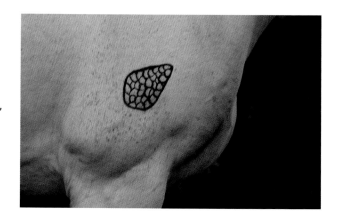

THYROID GLAND

The main function of the thyroid gland is to convert iodine from food into thyroxine. It also:
- controls the metabolic rate by burning calories
- promotes water loss through urine
- promotes protein synthesis
- influences growth, physical development and weight loss
- stimulates the breakdown of glycogen and glucose
- generates body heat.

Thyroxine increases in the blood during exercise and remains elevated for up to five hours. This means:
- more calories will be burned
- the heart will beat harder and faster
- appetite will increase
- digestion will become more active
- the horse will be more active and alert.

A deficit of thyroxine may result in decreased appetite, dull coat, delayed shedding, increased sensitivity to cold, lethargy and failure to produce milk in broodmares.

Fitter horses will have a higher metabolism than those on rest.

PARATHYROIDS

The parathyroid hormone (PTH) controls the level of calcium. This is essential for the bone strength and density, which allows the horse to withstand training and the physiological demands of competition.

Calcium is also the element that allows the normal conduction of electrical currents along nerves thus controlling how the nervous system works and how one nerve communicates with another. Brain function is dependent on calcium.

If calcium levels drop, the PTH causes:
- more calcium to be absorbed from bone
- the gut to absorb more calcium from food
- the kidneys to conserve calcium.

If calcium levels rise, the body stores more calcium in the bones and excretes more calcium in the urine.

Horses obtain most of their calcium from grass, hay and legumes within bagged feeds. Alfalfa is particularly high in calcium.

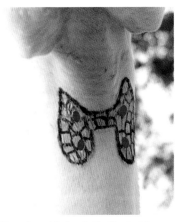

The Parathyroid glands (indicated by the red dots) actually lie hidden behind the thyroid gland.

PANCREAS

Located near the stomach this secretes digestive juices, insulin and glucagons, which control sugar levels in the blood and tissues. This is important in mobilising stored sugars creating extra energy sources during exercise and performance (see page 73).

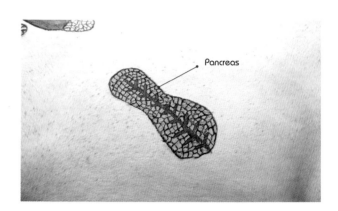

Pancreas

ADRENAL GLANDS

There are two adrenal glands, one on top of each kidney. The main hormones they secrete are cortisol, controlled by the pituitary gland and adrenalin controlled by the nervous system.

Cortisol, known as the main stress hormone, is secreted as a result of long lasting or chronic stress. This leads to increased production of glucose from proteins and fats, which is used to support the body in times of stress. However, extended recruitment of protein could be why more highly strung horses have less muscle bulk than their more relaxed counterparts. Cortisol also inhibits the inflammatory response that can lead to the pain and swelling of joints in arthritis and bursitis. Prolonged release, for example long term isolation, or travelling long distances with poor ventilation and limited access to water, may also compromise immune function resulting in increased susceptibility to disease.

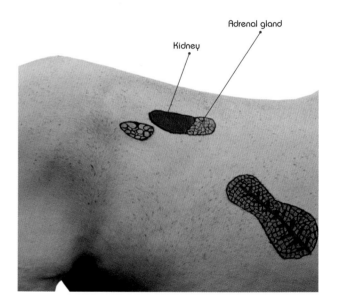

Adrenal gland

Kidney

Adrenalin is released in response to anxiety or fear. These emotions lead to autonomic nervous system activation and subsequent fuelling of the fight flight response. Aspects of this response controlled by adrenalin are dilation of the pupils, sweating and increased heart and respiration rates all in preparation for the ensuing action.

Adrenalin produced in physically exhilarating situations is known as the adrenalin rush which increases the amount of oxygen in the lungs which boosts physical performance for short bursts of time.

Part ten

During prolonged exercise, at competition or as exercise intensity increases, neural messages are sent to the adrenal glands which respond by secreting adrenalin into the bloodstream, helping to sustain high levels of exertion for longer.

OVARIES

The ovaries produce the two female hormones:
- **progesterone**, which prepares the uterus for implantation of the fertilised ovum, maintains pregnancy and promotes the development of the mammary glands, and
- **oestrogen** which is responsible for typical female sexual characteristics and lubrication of the genital tract (see page 143). The ovaries also produce a small amount of testosterone.

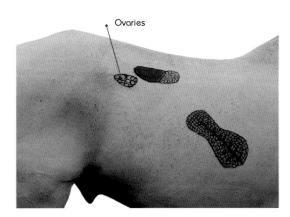

Ovaries

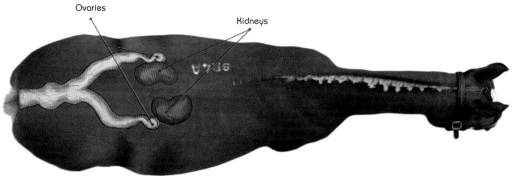

Ovaries

Kidneys

TESTES

These produce **testosterone** which is important for libido and the development and maintenance of male sex characteristics including muscle mass, condition, tone and strength. A small amount of testosterone is also produced by the adrenal glands. Once gelded, testosterone levels plummet, reducing female distractions and the urge to reproduce. This makes geldings generally more consistent in their behaviour, less temperamental, more complacent and more trainable than stallions. As testosterone, adrenalin and cortisol levels are higher in the morning, this is the best time to train.

The Endocrine System

ENDOCRINE TRAINING

Regular exercise stimulates the production of hormones for example cortisol, adrenalin, testosterone, growth hormone and endorphins, which are essential for wellbeing, exercise and training. The more circulating hormones there are in the blood, the more easily and effectively the horse will be able to exercise and the stronger he will become. This affects stamina, agility, courage and the ability to carry the weight of the rider.

A well conditioned endocrine system influences:
- **Physiological training**. This affects optimal functioning of the heart, lungs, gastrointestinal tract and the glands themselves.
- **Neuromuscular training**. This involves the muscles, fascia and tendons, as well as the brain, spine and nerves.
- **Psychological training**. A quiet relaxed state of mind enables a more effective and focussed response to training.

Conditioning the Endocrine System

Appropriate, structured exercise in preparation for an event prepares the horse to cope with the physical, emotional and mental stress of competition. Consistency, planning and preparation are the secrets to improvement and success. Endocrine training is accomplished through:

- Progressive exposure to a variety of situations to stimulate the production of adrenalin and cortisol. This can be achieved through experiences such as exposure to training shows, unforeseen situations when out hacking, outings in the lorry and even horse agility classes. This is the type of training undergone by police horses.
- Short bursts of high intensity, anaerobic exercise stimulates the production of testosterone, growth hormones, endorphins and thyroxin.
- Longer training sessions to condition the production of adrenalin and cortisol.

Overtraining and Fatigue

Overtraining can leave the horse anxious, depressed, low on energy and vulnerable to infections. The endocrine system can be stressed from:
- strenuous exercise or overzealous training without suitable rest periods
- a heavy competition schedule.

Reducing Endocrine Stress

Keeping the horse as calm and relaxed as possible helps to conserve the endocrine system for optimum performance and reduces the risk of endocrine fatigue.

- Training should proceed in progressive, regulated, incremental steps.

- In the run up to a big occasion, the last piece of fast fittening work should take place 7 days before the event to allow for a week of lighter work.

- Reduce travelling stress by stopping every couple of hours to give water. If the horse suffers from separation anxiety, take a pony companion if necessary.

- Maintain a good intake of water and electrolytes.

- For optimum performance and calm acceptance of training in young or inexperienced horses it is important to keep the horse as relaxed as possible. Introduce new lessons slowly in a calm environment.

- Practise a relaxed and happy state of mind. Avoid training if rider, trainer or horse is already stressed. One will pick up from the other! Always handle quietly and sensitively.

- Consider domestic management. A horse being bullied in a field or stabled next to an aggressive companion will become stressed or depressed.

Rest and Recovery

During and after strenuous exercise the pituitary gland produces chemicals that stimulate the release of adrenalin and cortisol into the blood. If the horse is continually expected to perform high intensity work or following demanding exercise such as a three day event, the endocrine system can take up to four weeks to rid the body of excess stress hormones and recover. As the initial 'high' recedes, it is not unusual for a horse to appear lethargic, disinterested in food or training or suffer digestional upsets. During this time, which varies from horse to horse, it is important to rest, recuperate and enjoy quiet hacks before gradually returning to work. Following recuperation after established fitness, the horse will recover and get stronger quicker.

SUMMARY

- The endocrine system is composed of glands distributed throughout the body.
- The hypothalamus works closely with the pituitary gland to maintain equilibrium within the body.
- Glands produce chemical substances called hormones.
- Hormones affect every aspect of training and behaviour.
- Adrenalin is important for exercise performance.
- Conditioning the endocrine system increases the amount and efficiency of hormones produced.

The urinary system filters the blood,

controls the amount of fluid in the body

and removes harmful waste.

The Urinary System

THE URINARY SYSTEM

The urinary system consists of the kidneys and the ureters, bladder and urethra. It plays an important role in homeostasis and is responsible for eliminating waste from the body. The kidneys regulate the blood by filtration, reabsorption and secretion.

Homeostasis

Homeostasis, controlled by the autonomic nervous system (see page 110) and the endocrine system (see page 122), monitors internal balance and can be easily upset by exercise, stress and disease. It is the body's ability to adjust its internal environment to maintain a stable equilibrium with regards to:

• nutrient levels
• hydration
• blood levels including blood pressure, volume and concentration
• temperature.

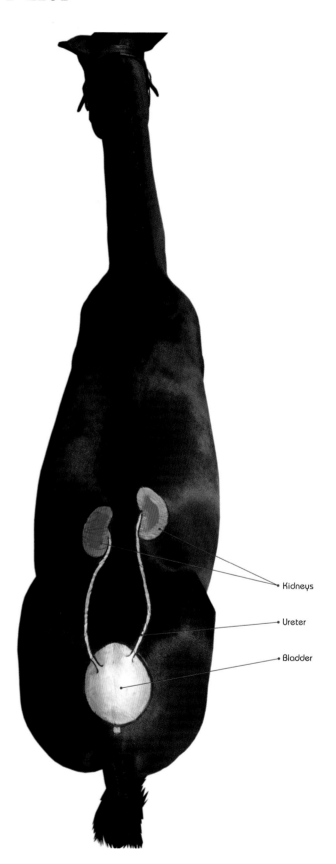

Kidneys

Ureter

Bladder

Part eleven

THE KIDNEYS

Kidney Function

As an organ of detoxification, the kidneys cleanse the blood, remove toxins and excrete the liquid waste as urine, which is carried by the ureters to the bladder where it is stored until evacuated through the urethra. It does this by:

- maintaining correct fluid levels
- eliminating toxic substances such as urea and ammonia
- filtering plasma
- regulating electrolyte levels within the blood
- maintaining a constant blood concentration by regulating the loss of water
- regulating blood alkali/acidity levels
- releasing hormones through the adrenal glands which are part of the endocrine system (see page 128) to:
  - regulate blood volume
  - manage calcium levels
  - regulate blood pressure through the enzyme rennin
- regulating blood glucose and amino acid levels.

Kidney Structure

The kidneys weigh approximately 700 grams each and are 15cm in length. The right, bean shaped kidney lies beneath the ribs of the last 2 or 3 thoracic and first lumbar vertebrae and the left heart shaped kidney lies beneath the last rib of the thoracic and first 2 or 3 lumbar vertebrae. Each kidney is enveloped by a 'kidney capsule' of dense fibrous tissue. They are held in place by the surrounding organs, the dense fibrous renal fascia and are well protected by the transverse processes and a collection of fat which often surrounds them. The renal nerves, arteries, veins, lymphatic vessels and ureter enter or leave the kidney at an indentation known as the hilus. The renal cortex, the outer portion of the kidney, consists of a mass of millions of tightly packed tubes known as nephrons or kidney tubules. Each nephron begins with a cup shaped Bowman's capsule and is an individual filtration unit. These are the functional components of the kidney.

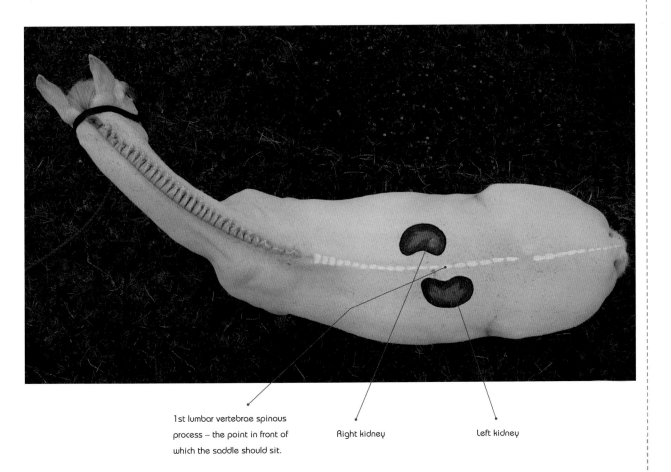

1st lumbar vertebrae spinous process – the point in front of which the saddle should sit.

Right kidney

Left kidney

How Kidneys Work

Kidney function is extremely complex.

- Blood is brought directly from the aorta to the kidney by the renal artery which continually divides until it becomes many millions of tangled clusters of capillaries each known as a glomerulus.
- Plasma, containing water, platelets, glucose, urea, hormones and enzymes, vitamins and minerals, is forced from the capillaries of the glomerulus under pressure into the Bowman's capsule. The red blood cells and normal protein molecules, too large to be filtered out, remain in the capillaries.
- The liquid is then forced from the Bowman's capsule through the various parts of the nephron. Here, the descending and ascending limbs of the loop of Henle and distal tubule filter out salts, reabsorb water from renal tubules and maintain the correct balance of water in the body. 99% of water is reabsorbed with only 1% being excreted as urine. The most concentrated urine is found in the bottom of each loop.
- The liquid returns to the renal cortex in the distal tubule and from there it continues into the collecting duct where it trickles into the renal pelvis which narrows to become the ureter.
- Urine is moved along the ureters, which have a mucus lining to prevent reabsorption, by peristalsis.

- Filtered blood collected from the loop of Henle is removed from the kidneys and returned to the blood stream via the renal vein.
  Between 1000 and 2000 litres of blood is filtered through the kidneys up to 60 times a day.

Each kidney has 3 parts, the renal cortex, medulla and pelvis

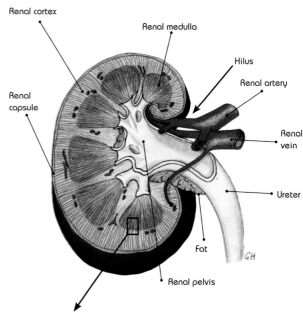

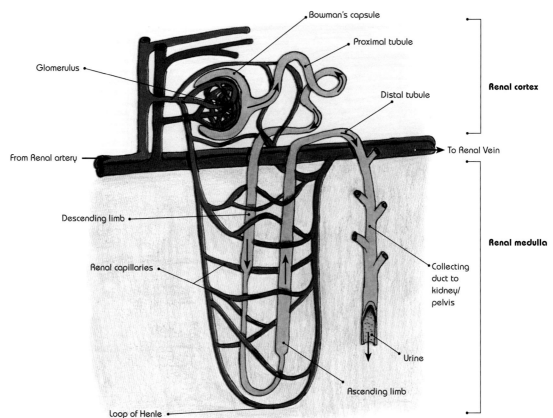

BLADDER

The bladder with an approximate volume of 4.5 litres is a storage unit for urine which continually drains from the kidneys. It has enormous capacity to stretch. A horse will produce 5 to 15 litres of urine per day depending on hydration. Water is taken in by drinking, eating grass, haylage, soaked hay or feeds and as a by-product of respiration. It is excreted by urinating, sweating, breathing out and in faeces.

The bladder is lined with a mucous membrane which coats and protects the wall and prevents the reabsorption urine.

When the bladder is full, sensory receptors send messages to the central nervous system which sends motor neuron messages to the bladder to contract and the sphincter muscle to relax. Urine can then exit via the urethra. This process occurs due to co-ordinated activity of voluntary and involuntary elements of the nervous system. In stallions and geldings the urethra is long as it runs through the penis. Urine is propelled along by muscle contraction. In mares, the short urethra empties into the vestibule at the back of the vagina. It is then forced out through the vulva.

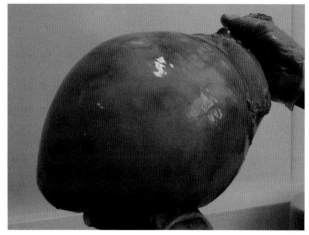

A full bladder

Urine

Urine, containing nitrogen, salts, excess sugars, and other substances that are filtered out of the bloodstream, is a thick, yellowy, syrupy liquid. It is cloudy due to suspended calcium carbonate crystals. It is composed of 96% water, 2% urea, 2% salts, some bile pigments and some hormones.

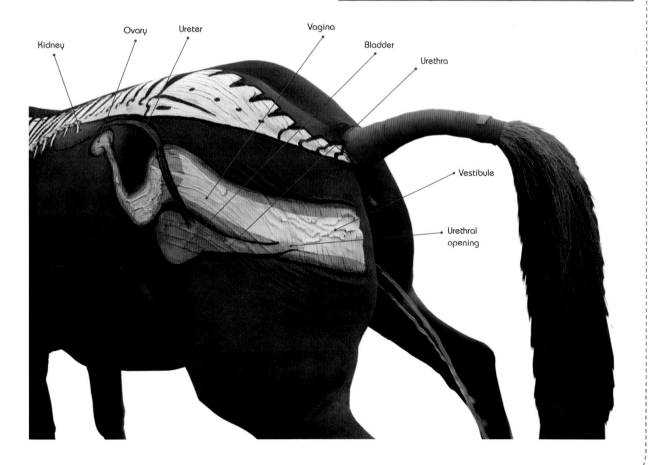

Kidney · Ovary · Ureter · Vagina · Bladder · Urethra · Vestibule · Urethral opening

BLOOD PRESSURE, EXERCISE AND HYDRATION

How the Kidneys Influence Blood Pressure

The kidneys are the most important organs for the long term control of blood pressure. When blood pressure is low they release the hormone rennin which increases blood pressure by:

• constricting the blood vessels. This is known as vasoconstriction.
• reabsorbing salt from urine back into the blood.

Effect of Exercise on the Kidneys

During exercise the kidneys reabsorb more water which helps to keep blood pressure high by delivering more oxygen and energy to the muscle cells and replacing the loss of fluid from sweating. They also secrete the enzyme rennin which diverts blood away from the kidneys thus making a higher volume of blood available for the muscles.

How the Kidneys Regulate Hydration

Adequate water intake is essential to keep the kidneys working well, flush toxins from vital organs, carry nutrients to every cell and remove waste products and excess nutrients in the urine. Water levels are altered by increasing or decreasing the flow of urine and controlling normal levels of sodium and other electrolytes. When there is an excess of water, the kidneys filter it from the blood and produce more copious amounts of urine. If a horse is dehydrated, sensory cells in the hypothalamus trigger the pituitary gland to secrete antidiuretic hormone which causes more water to be reabsorbed within the kidneys so producing less but more concentrated urine (see page 136). It also triggers the sensation of thirst. With just 3% dehydration, performance suffers.

Health and the Urinary System

Infections of the urinary system are very uncommon in horses. Initial indications of infection or inflammation are urine discolouration or mucus in the urine. If this occurs it is important to call the vet.

Normal Water Intake

• 5–7 gallons per day for a resting horse
• Up to 20 gallons per day for long hard exercise.

The Importance of Electrolytes

The primary electrolytes are sodium and potassium chloride, bicarbonate, calcium, phosphorus and magnesium. They are important in maintaining homeostasis, the transmission of nerve impulses, and the healthy function of the muscles and the circulatory system. Electrolytes are lost in sweat which in horses has a higher concentration of electrolytes than in humans. These need to be replaced. Electrolyte balance and hydration go hand in hand.

Electrolytes are lost:
• during periods of training or intense performance. Sweating begins after 10 minutes of exercise.
• in high temperatures and high humidity when horses can lose 10–15 litres per hour which equates to 100 litres in a 10-hour endurance race!
• when travelling long distances
• in urine.

In order to maintain a healthy electrolyte balance, fresh water must be accessible at all times and electrolytes should be added to feed. Progressive dehydration and loss of electrolytes eliminates the stimulus to trigger thirst and by not drinking, a horse worsens his dehydration problem.

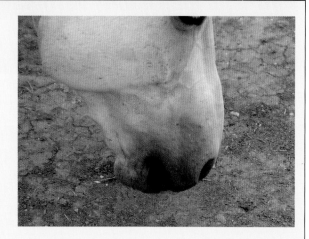

A deficiency in electrolytes can lead to dehydration, tying up, muscle fatigue, lethargy, constipation or decreased performance. Sodium chloride or common table salt is the most important electrolyte. If the horse is deficient he will lick soil in order to replenish it. A horse should have access to a salt lick. Too much salt can result in dehydration.

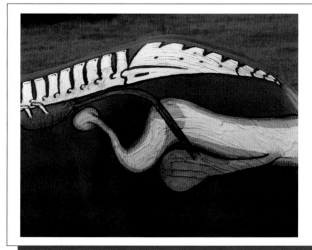

SUMMARY

• The urinary system cleanses the blood and excretes waste products such as urea, ammonia and toxins.
• The urinary system plays an important role in homeostasis.
• The kidneys rely on a rich blood supply to function effectively.
• A healthy horse will excrete 5–15 litres of urine per day.
• The kidneys play a vital part in balancing blood pressure.
• Electrolyte balance is key to regulating hydration.

The Urinary System

Reproduction, the miracle of birth,

ensures the survival of the species.

The Reproductive System

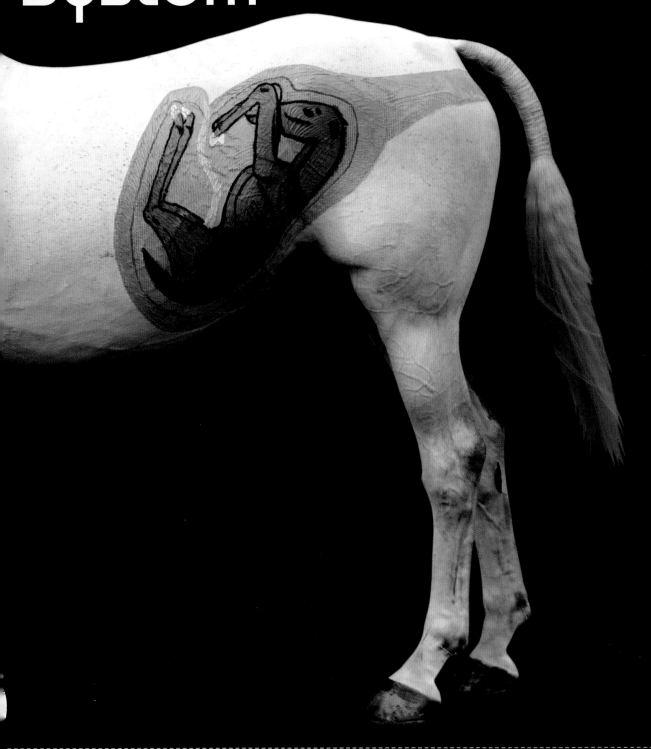

REPRODUCTION

There are still some areas in the world where horses run in herds and reproduction is a case of survival of the fittest. In the modern domesticated horse, the onus of selective reproduction falls to horse owners and the mating process is engineered, often to produce specifically desired characteristics, rather than spontaneous. Modern breeding practices can increase the rate of conception, healthy pregnancy and successful foaling. However, if not used wisely they can also produce too many unwanted foals.

THE STALLION

The male reproductive anatomy consists of the testes, the scrotum, accessory glands and the penis.

Testes

Testes, which are oval in shape, generally reach their full size, about the size of a goose egg, by the time the horse is 2 years old. Once mature, they produce sperm and testosterone, the main male hormone which influences physical characteristics (see page 129). Sperm production takes 50–60 days and is produced in waves to ensure a constant supply. Stallions that ejaculate more often produce more sperm. Once produced, the sperm passes into the vas deferens, a muscular tube which propels the sperm and associated fluids into the urethra as the stallion ejaculates.

Scrotum

The testes are suspended in the scrotum, which at 4–7°C cooler than within the body are located externally to ensure the correct temperature for sperm development.

With its loose skin it is designed to lose heat when the external temperature is warm and to be pulled up against the body by the cremaster muscle for warmth when it is cold.

Accessory Glands

The vesicular, prostate and bulbourethral glands produce the semen in which the sperm is suspended and account for 60–80% of the total volume of ejaculate.

Penis

The internal portion of the penis consists of erectile tissue which becomes engorged with blood and will enlarge by 50% when the stallion is aroused. The penis is encased within the sheath and lubricated by smegma produced from a sinus near the tip of the penis. It is important that the penis is kept clean as excessive smegma can harbour infection. It is also important it is only washed with water as antibacterial cleansers will kill the protective microbes.

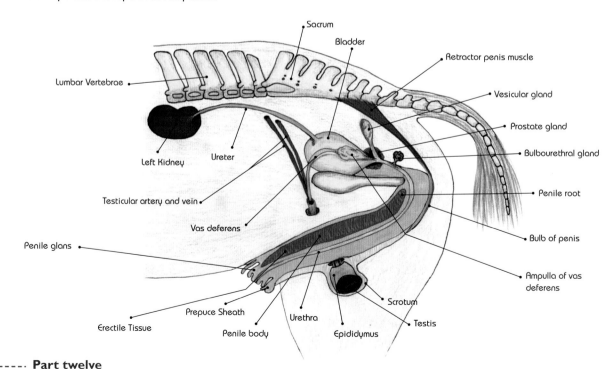

THE MARE

The female reproductive anatomy consists of the ovaries, fallopian tubes, uterus, vagina and vulva.

Ovaries

The ovaries, about the size of an egg, are located under and protected by the lumbar vertebrae. A filly at birth is born with a full complement of eggs. One egg is released during each cycle commencing during the horse's second year. The ovaries also produce the female sex hormones oestrogen and progesterone. Oestrogen is responsible for the release of eggs and behavioural changes associated with in-season mares. If fertilisation occurs, then progesterone maintains pregnancy.

Fallopian Tubes

These narrow twisted tubes, about 2–3mm in diameter and 20–30cm in length are lined with cilla. If the mare has mated and sperm are present, the released egg will be fertilised here. It is then moved along the tube to the uterus by peristalsis and wafting of cilia. Unfertilised eggs disintegrate in the fallopian tubes.

Uterus

The uterus, the largest of the female sex organs, is a Y- shaped tube with a hollow uterine body and 2 horns which are a continuation of fallopian tubes. The embryo develops in the uterus which is capable of enormous expansion as the foetus grows. It is housed and nourished within the uterus in the amniotic sac. The uterus is lined with strong muscles which push the foal into the birth canal at parturition.

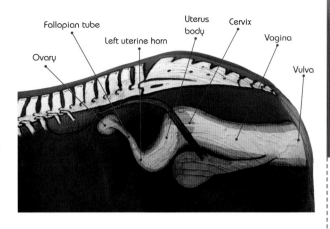

Cervix

The cervix, about 4cm in diameter and 6cm long, forms the neck of the womb. When the mare is not in season and during pregnancy, this is tightly closed to prevent infection. It is very elastic and dilates rapidly just before parturition to allow the foal to enter the vagina at birth.

Vagina

The vagina, about 15–20cm long has an extremely muscular wall lined with mucus to allow the penis to penetrate and the foal to be born.

Vulva

The vulva is the external opening of the vagina and consists of two labia or lips and the clitoris. It lies underneath the anus.

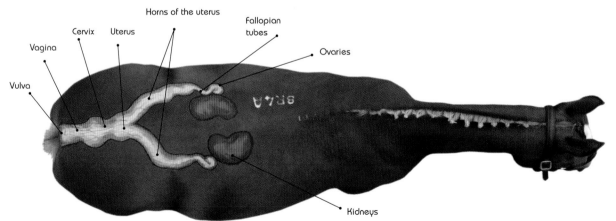

The mare has 2 ovaries. In this picture their location in relation to the saddle is clear. At certain times within the oestrous cycle the ovaries can contribute to muscle soreness in the lumbar region.

Oestrus Cycle

The oestrous cycle is governed by hormones released from the hypothalamus and pituitary gland. The mare's cycle generally takes 21 days and is only active between the months of March and September when day length is greater. The gestation period for a mare is 11 months. This means the foal is born in the warmer months of plenty between March and August. The mare is only receptive to the stallion for 5 of these days and ovulation usually takes place during the last 2 days.

When the mare is coming into heat she may lose concentration, be unwilling to move forward during exercise or be oversensitive and flighty. She will often become restless, irritable, show mild signs of colic, raise her tail and 'wink' the vulva. She may also frequently pass small amounts of bright yellow urine. This often causes stallions to display the flehmen's posture (see page 81) in response to the pheromones in the urine.

PREGNANCY AND BIRTH

Riding and Managing the Pregnant Mare

- The first few days of pregnancy are the most critical.
- Fit, healthy, strong mares can be ridden up to the last month of pregnancy. After the fourth month the mare will find it difficult to collect and bend and it is unwise to jump as pregnancy advances.
- A calm environment, sensible nutrition and foot care, worming, vaccinations and regular exercise will help ensure a healthy pregnancy and trouble free birth.

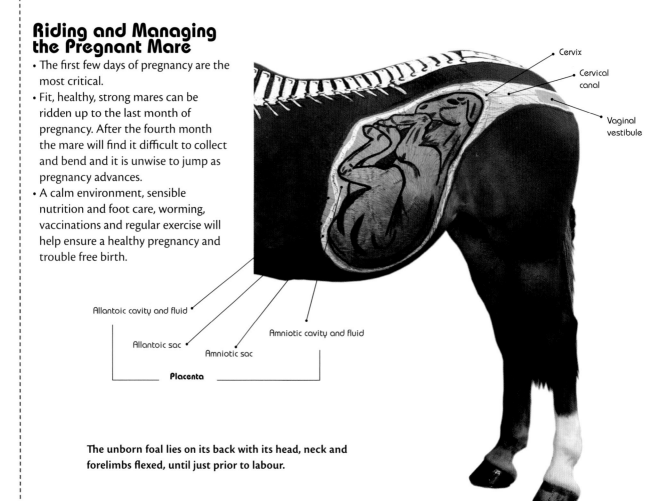

Cervix

Cervical canal

Vaginal vestibule

Allantoic cavity and fluid

Amniotic cavity and fluid

Allantoic sac

Amniotic sac

Placenta

The unborn foal lies on its back with its head, neck and forelimbs flexed, until just prior to labour.

Stages of foetal development

Week	Approximate Length	Some features of foetus development
1	–	Following conception foetal cells divide rapidly. Nutrient is derived initially from uterine secretions and then the yolk sac.
3	1.5cm	As the foetus floats in the amniotic sac the head, buds for eyes, tail and legs begin to emerge. At the end of the fourth week the foetal heartbeat may be detected.
6	2.5cm	The foetus attaches to the uterus lining, the head becomes more recognisable and the skull starts to emerge along with rudimentary eyelids, nostrils, stifle and hock joints.
8	3.5cm	The placenta begins to develop, its role is to provide the life giving blood supply and remove waste products. The head becomes more domed as the skull becomes more distinct. The ribs begin to form and short legs evolve.
9	6cm	Oxygen and soluble food provided by the mare via the placenta are exchanged for urea and carbon dioxide. The thickness of placenta means that large antibody molecules cannot pass through. Hooves form and the foetus begins to resemble a horse!
12	12cm	The spine becomes more evident and outward sex characteristics form.
15	18cm	Some hair develops, the ears begin to unfurl and coronary bands form.
22	30cm	Development continues with more and more features emerging. The foetus is about the size of a rabbit.
32	70cm	All the features become more distinct.
44	115cm	The foetus is now covered with hair, has a short tail, fully developed lungs and strengthened legs. It is about the size of a large dog.
48		The foal is ready to be born.

Approaching Birth

Milk appears in the udder 2–4 weeks before birth.
Several days before birth:

- relaxation of the vulva may alter the mare's tail position
- enlargement of and clear waxy coating will appear on the teats
- milk will begin to drip or squirt
- the mare may be nervous and restless and show signs similar to mild colic, lying down and rolling
- frequent defecation and squatting will take place.

Most mares foal either late at night or in the early hours of the morning, often when spectators are not present! This implies mares have some influence over parturition timing perhaps to ensure a safe arrival time when fewer predators are about.

Labour

There are 3 stages of labour:

Stage 1

Uterine contractions push the foal into the rapidly dilating cervix. The foal turns onto his front and extends his head, neck and forelimbs into a position to fit through the cervical canal. The mare begins to strain. The forelimbs burst through the allantoic sac, the water bag, releasing allantoic fluid.

Stage 2

The mare lies down and the abdominal muscles strain as the vagina widens. The front feet appear followed by the nose and shoulders. The amniotic sac ruptures and the foal starts to breathe. Strong abdominal contractions continue until hind legs emerge.

Stage 3

As the mare gets up, the umbilical cord breaks. Within the first 30 minutes the foal makes several unsteady attempts to stand and searches for the udder. The mare licks the foal's anus to stimulate the passing of meconium. The placenta is expelled about 1 hour after birth.

Post-natal

A newborn foal receives protective antibodies in colostrum, the mare's first milk. These lose their efficacy at 4–5 months, by which time the foal is providing independent protection.

Following Birth

- Mares can be ridden when the foal is three months.
- To ensure the foal gets the nourishment and vitamins necessary for a good start in life and to reduce the risk of separation anxiety, ulcers and weight loss, the foal should be kept with the mare as long as possible
- The best time to reintroduce the mare to work is when the foal is weaned at about 7½ months.
- It is important to bring the mare back into work slowly taking care to tone and strengthen core postural, abdominal and pelvic stabiliser muscles (see page 45) weakened by pregnancy (see page 144).

Breeding

Practical and ethical considerations to take into account are:
• time and financial liabilities
• physical health of the mare
• the purpose for which the foal is being bred
• the market in the event that the foal cannot be kept
• the owner's expertise. Can he or she properly manage the mare through gestation and birth?
• whether the owner has the expertise to properly manage and train a foal once it is born.

Techniques such as embryo transfer and artificial insemination are now readily available. This allows a greater choice of stallions and dams, better selection procedures, decreased risk of injury to humans, mares or stallions, decreased risk of disease and an increased chance of genetic improvement.

The adult horse has 64 chromosomes, 32 from each parent. These can combine in any configuration, thus making breeding a gamble. Selecting strong stallions and mares with suitable genetic histories and desirable temperaments can increase the chance of a well proportioned, healthy, athletic foal. Although tempting, breeding from a mare for emotional reasons, because she is lame, temperamental, is not performing as the owner would like, has poor conformation or a weakness is not advisable.

SUMMARY
• In the modern horse reproduction is largely engineered rather than spontaneous.
• The male reproductive anatomy consists of the testes, the scrotum, accessory glands and the penis.
• The female reproductive anatomy consists of the ovaries, fallopian tubes, uterus, vagina and vulva.
• Modern reproduction techniques increase genetic improvement and lessen the risk of disease.
• It is important to consider the purpose for which the foal is being bred.

PAINTING HORSES

The paint that is used on the horses is water based, non toxic and completely harmless.

All of the paintings are designed and painted on the horse by the author. It takes between 4 and 6 hours to paint a horse depending on the complexity of the anatomical system.

All diagrams in the book are hand drawn by the author.

Most of the paint rubs off with a rubber curry comb, and the remainder washes off with warm water.

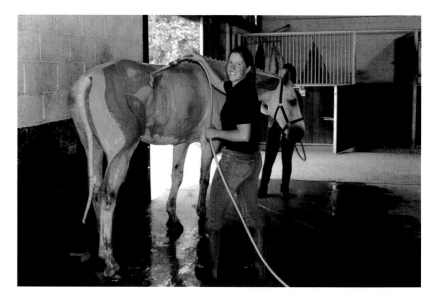

UNDERSTANDING TERMINOLOGY

Adipose – fatty tissue

Amygdala – the part of the brain involved in processing emotions, especially anger and fear

Antigens – foreign substances such as bacteria, viruses and other toxins

Axon – the long part of a neuron or nerve fibre that conducts impulses away from the body of a cell

Caudal – towards the tail

Cell body – this contains the nucleus and mitochondria, really important for energy production

Cilia – tiny hair like projections that move in a Mexican wave like motion

Collagen – the fibrous protein constituent of bone, cartilage, tendon and other connective tissue

Cranial – towards the head

Cryotherapy – the use of cold to remove heat from a body part

Dendrites – fibres of brain and nerve cells that receive signals from other brain and nerve cells

Distal – furthest from the centre

Dorsal – towards the back

Electrolytes – minerals, mainly salts, that are dissolved in fluid

Fight or flight – an early evolutionary behaviour strategy to deal with dangerous and unexpected situations

Glycogen – a type of carbohydrate stored in the liver and muscle cells that is easily converted to glucose to meet metabolic energy needs

Hives – a skin condition characterised by itching welts caused by an allergic reaction

Homeostasis – internal stability or equilibrium

Hypothalamus – control centre for the autonomic nervous system regulating functions such as sleep, body temperature and appetite. Also acts as an endocrine gland controlling hormonal secretions of the pituitary gland.

Keratin – the chief structural constituent of hair, nails, horns and hooves

Lymphocyte – a white blood cell that plays an important role in defending the body against disease

Medulla oblongata – the part of the hindbrain that controls autonomic functions such as breathing, digestion and heart rate

Meninges – the three membranes that cover and surround the brain and spinal cord

Mitochondria – parts of cells responsible for energy production

Neuron – nerve cells responsible for controlling reactions from the senses, mood, thoughts and emotions

Neurotransmitter – a chemical substance that transmits nerve impulses across the spaces between nerve cells or neurons

Olfactory – relating to the sense of smell

Peristalsis – movement of contents along a tubular structure by wave like muscular contractions

pH scale – measure of the degree of the acidity or the alkalinity of a solution on a scale of 0 to 14. Water is 7

Phagocyte – a white blood cell that engulfs and absorbs harmful micro organisms and waste material from the blood and other tissues

Pheromone – a chemical substance secreted to influence the behaviour of another member of the same species

Plexus – a network of nerves

Protein – a fundamental component, including substances such as enzymes, hormones and antibodies, essential for the proper functioning of all living cells

Protraction – reaching forward, the forward swing of the stride

Receptor – an organ or cell, which can transmit a signal to a sensory nerve in response to light, heat or other external stimuli

Retraction – the backward push of the stride

Subcutaneous – the third and deepest layer of skin

Swann cells – these fatty cells increase the speed at which signals can travel along axons

Synthesis – the combining of separate parts to produce a more complex product

Vascular – relating to vessels that circulate fluids

Vasoconstriction – the constriction of blood vessels, which reduces blood flow

Vasodilation – the dilation of blood vessels, which increases blood flow

Ventral – towards the underside

ABOUT THE AUTHOR

GILLIAN HIGGINS is an equine and human sports and remedial therapist, event rider and coach with a passion for equine anatomy and anatomical art. As a leading expert in her field she founded **Horses Inside Out.** This unique organisation gives riders, trainers, students and therapists a fascinating insight into the training, management, comfort and welfare of their horses through understanding anatomy, physiology and biomechanics. With an enthusiastic style of presentation and the ability to bring her subject to life, Gillian is in demand worldwide. Gillian runs courses in anatomy and biomechanics, dissections for therapists, massage and stretching for horse owners as well as day courses for colleges and universities and evening lecture demonstrations for all. She has written several books incuding:

- *Pilates and Stretching for Horses*
- *The Horses Inside Out Anatomy Poster Book*
- *How Your Horse Moves*

and DVDs:

- *Movement from the Anatomical Perspective*
- *Pilates for Horses*

STEPHANIE MARTIN has been involved with horses from a very early age and has a particular interest in their welfare. With a keen interest in literature, and a 'way with words', she has written various articles for many magazines and has played a valuable part in putting together the text for this book.

Acknowledgments

I would like to thank my father **DAVID HIGGINS** for the photographs, painting assistance, IT support, humour, endless patience and wisdom. Thanks also to my friends and mentors Andrew and Catherine Hemmings who have given their time painstakingly reading through the manuscript. Thank you to my friend Fiona Davidson for riding and allowing me to paint her horses, as well as all my other friends who have helped in one valuable way or another. Finally, special praise and extra carrots go to Freddie Fox, the star of *Horses Inside Out* and the main model for this book!

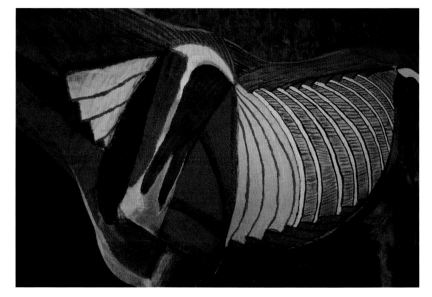

INDEX

This book is dedicated to horses everywhere

A DAVID AND CHARLES BOOK
© David and Charles, Ltd 2012

David and Charles is an imprint of David and Charles, Ltd
Suite A, Tourism House, Pynes Hill, Exeter, EX2 5WS

Text and designs copyright © Gillian Higgins 2012

All Photography © Gillian Higgins except –
P5 and BL p134 – Helen Richmond Photography; B p14, BL p43, BR
p48, BR p128 – Horse Pix; B p19, M p20, T p23, TR p37, BL p41, B p44,
B p54, TR p65 – David & Charles; TR p106 – Paula Lee; P146 – Warren
Photographic

First published in the UK and US in 2012
Digital edition published in 2012

Layout of digital editions may vary depending on
reader hardware and display settings.

Gillian Higgins has asserted the right to be identified as
author of this work in accordance with the Copyright,
Designs and Patents Act, 1988.

A catalogue record for this book is available from the
British Library.

ISBN-13: 9781446300961 hardback

15 14 13

MIX
Paper | Supporting
responsible forestry
FSC® C020056

Acquisitions Editor: Neil Baber
Senior Editor: Verity Muir
Project Editor: Nicola Moffatt
Senior Designer: Jodie Lystor
Production Manager: Beverley Richardson

This edition printed in China by Leo Paper Products
Ltd for:
David and Charles, Ltd
Suite A, Tourism House, Pynes Hill, Exeter, EX2 5WS

David and Charles publishes high-quality books on
a wide range of subjects. For more information visit
www.davidandcharles.com.

Follow us on Facebook and Instagram by searching
for @dandcbooks.

Layout of the digital edition of this book may vary
depending on reader hardware and display settings.

LOVED THIS BOOK?

Here are some others you may enjoy...

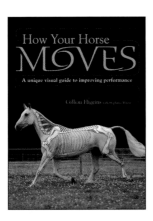

How Your Horse Moves
Gillian Higgins with Stephanie Martin
ISBN-13: 978-1-4463-0099-2

Take a fresh look at equine anatomy and biomechanics with this graphic guide to how horses move, presented from the inside out.

Essential Horse Health
Kieran O'Brien
ISBN-13: 978-0-7153-2542-1

A book that deals with everything likely to go wrong with your horse, in enough depth to make it indispensable for all horse owners.

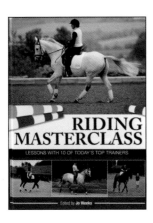

Riding Masterclass
Edited by Jo Weeks
ISBN-13: 978-0-7153-2915-3

Add professional polish to your skills with this collection of lessons from the elite trainers of the equestrian world.

101 Schooling Exercises for Horse and Rider
Compiled by
Jaki Bell with Andrew Day
ISBN-13: 978-0-7153-1950-5

You'll never be stuck for schooling ideas again with this collection of 101 exercises to choose from.